Love on a Leash

Liz Palika

Alpine
Blue Ribbon Books
Loveland, Colorado

Love on a Leash
Copyright © 1996 by Liz Palika.

Library of Congress Cataloging-in-Publication Data

Palika, Liz 1954–
    Love on a leash : choosing, training, and certifying a therapy dog / Liz Palika.
      p. cm.
    Includes bibliographical references.
    ISBN 0-931866-76-6
    1. Dogs—Therapeutic use   I. Title.
    RM931.A65P35 1996   94-3877
    636.7'088--dc20   CIP

This book is available at special quantity discounts to organizations, clubs, or for premiums or educational use. Contact the publisher for details.

1 2 3 4 5 6 7 8 9 0

Cover design: B. J. McKinney
Cover photo: Liz Palika. Andrew Paul visits with his friend, Mandy.

All photos taken by the author except as noted.

Text design: Cat Ohala and Harlene Finn
Text layout: Harlene Finn

Printed in the United States of America.

Many manufacturers secure trademark rights for their products. When Alpine Publications is aware of a trademark claim, we print the product name in initial capital letters or as trademarked.

Contents

Dedicated to the memory of my maternal grandparents,
Roland Daniel Brown and Melba Stanard Brown.
Their patience and love taught me to love
and respect my elders.

And to Care Bear, a wonderful Australian Shepherd,
the ultimate therapy dog, whose sole purpose
in life is to love people.

Foreword

Why should we use animals as a part of therapy? Two words explain it all: unconditional love. Those who are ill, disabled, elderly, and those who must live or stay at a care facility or in an institution are often deprived of acceptance, love, or touch. Therapy dogs provide these necessities of life.

Care Bear, Hugs, Jupiter, Gracie, and Zippy (among thousands of other certified therapy dogs) mind little that Mrs. Baker, who no longer speaks, was once a world-renowned opera singer. The dogs don't care that the General, who now says only "Good dog," once commanded a division of soldiers or that Mr. Hall prefers not to wear his false teeth and likes to wear a sweater with holes in the pockets. The dogs provide love—pure and simple.

Liz Palika is an expert on dogs, dog training, and therapy work. For more than four years she has been my teacher, my mentor, and my friend. Through her efforts, tens of thousands of people have been touched with canine love and educated about their best friends. Through her efforts in organizing and coordinating countless "visits," an elderly citizen who hadn't spoken in years began to talk, an angry ninety-year-old woman in a care facility now makes sure she's dressed and ready for the dogs. Another resident has mailed photos of Liz's therapy dog group to family members across the country so that her family and friends can see her dog friends. Few of us have the patience to share so much, but Liz makes up in patience what those of us lack.

Sometimes I still smile thinking back to that day when my rambunctious terrier, Zippy, and I graduated from a beginners dog training class. Liz said, "Why don't you try one visit? She'll be great." Oh sure, I thought, as this year-old ball of energy raced around my feet, bouncing and barking. With Liz's confidence, I took that first step. Liz taught me that therapy dogs don't have to be furry little robots. They can have fun and they can make residents laugh with their antics.

So call it peer pressure or simply that I didn't know my high-energy pup, but Zippy is a wonderful therapy dog. She adores seniors. When invited, she snuggles down on beds, gives kisses, does tricks that rival a circus act, and struts through a care facility (as the cliché goes) like she owns the joint!

Animal-assisted therapy benefits the residents of care facilities. There are clinical studies that prove it. The dogs love being with the people they visit, too. Yet, little has been said about the efforts of the visit on the volunteers. Now, after logging more than 500 volunteer hours, I've discovered that I'm hooked on "visiting." I'm not alone. The other volunteers say the same, often teasing that it's more therapy for us than for the residents we visit.

Visiting makes one smile a little brighter, stand a little taller, and weep a little more easily. It's sheer pleasure when a warm tail-wagging hello stops a resident from crying or encourages someone to get out of bed. It's a slicing pain when someone passes away, but knowing that life was made easier by a visit, and perhaps warming a heart along the way, makes up for the personal sorrow.

Just as not all people have the right personality to volunteer, not all dogs have the temperament to be therapy dogs. Even after a few visits, you may still be concerned that your own dog might not be that idealized perfect little robot dog. Should this happen, just remember Zippy. She'll never be a robot; she'll always act like a dog, because that is exactly what she is. But boy, can she make people laugh!

Love on a Leash gives you all the tips, methods, and techniques for choosing, training, and working with a therapy dog, as well as information on how to make a visit a success. Read it, digest it, and then give it a try. Let Liz Palika's advice be your guide as you, too, take that first step. You might discover, as I did with Zippy, that you have a four-footed therapist ready and waiting to share miraculous canine love.

Eva Shaw
Vice President
Foundation for Pet Provided Therapy

Preface

Years ago, when I started doing therapy dog work, there were very few guidelines for people interested in this field. Sure, those of us who owned dogs knew how important our dogs were to us, both physically and emotionally, but when we wanted to share our dogs with others, very little information was available. Those of us who wanted to do this work really had to find our own way.

Today, however, researchers are studying many aspects of the relationship between pets (especially dogs) and people, and the results are astounding. Our dogs can help us stay healthy; can aid in recovery from injuries, illness, and surgery; and can even help us live longer.

I wrote this book for everyone who is thinking about therapy dog work. Is it right for you, personally? How much time do you need to devote to it? Is your dog suited for therapy dog work? What training will your dog need? How do you get started? What is certification and how do you get it? What is a therapy dog visit like? What are you expected to do during a visit? These and many other questions are answered in detail.

Additional information is provided for facilities considering adding a resident therapy dog. Discussed are the preparations needed prior to getting a dog, the training the dog will need, and how to use the dog so that the residents benefit from his presence.

Also included are the names and addresses of the national organizations that certify therapy dogs, as well as regional and local groups that organize visits. An extensive bibliography provides additional reading for those interested in the field.

I have found therapy dog work to be a rewarding volunteer activity. I have made *many* friends during my visits—both residents and staff members. My dogs love it and eagerly anticipate each visit. When a child hugs one of my dogs and whispers secrets in his ear, I melt inside. When a family member tells me how much their grandparent looked forward to our visit, when my dogs and I can make someone smile or, better yet, laugh, I know what we do is important.

Acknowledgments

Many people helped make this book possible, and I thank you all. Thank you first to the southern California chapter of the Love on a Leash Therapy Dog Program, Inc., in Oceanside, California, including:

Eva Shaw and Zippy, Welsh Terrier
Pam Posey and Gracie, Basset Hound
Laurie Blaisdell and Australian Shepherds Sam and Ditto
Sandy Dutweiler and Twigs, All American
Lauren Seals and Mandy, All American, and Tippi, Bishon Frise
Michelle Lund and Hugs, Australian Shepherd
Jeri Klosson and Poodles Amiga, Chica, and Topo
Velma Shirley and Dreyfuss, All American
Linda A. and Linda L. Schulte, and Border Collies Mouse and Clio
Sue Mertens and Tara and Fire, Irish Setters
Joan Swanson and Wayne Hamilton and their Golden Retrievers
    DC, Missy, and Shanna, and their Newfoundland Kody
Rich and Toni Schickel and their Labrador Misty
Bonnie Zobell and Jupiter, Golden Retriever

Thanks also to the following students, who posed for photograph after photograph:

Tony Castellano and his Weimaraners Joey and Jazzy
Jane Manion and her Weimaraners Emily and Wilma
Miles Dupriest and his litter of baby Australian Shepherds
Katherine Cleary and Junior, Australian Shepherd
Kathie Ogden and her dogs, including Travis and Steeler
Rachel Amado and her Dalmation Sparky

If I have forgotten anyone, please forgive me. It was not intentional.

Zippy, a Welsh Terrier, shares some love and affection with Velma Shirley. Zippy is certified by the Foundation for Pet Provided Therapy.

How Strong Is the Pet–People Bond?

The Power of Pets

As long as I can remember, dogs were a part of my life. The first dog I remember was Molly, an English Setter, who was supposed to be my grandfather's dog, but followed my grandmother everywhere she went. I have a Norman Rockwell-type memory of my grandmother rocking in her chair on the porch of their old three-story house in Connecticut, Molly at her feet. Jack, a big black dog of uncertain parentage, was next. He was great, because he always played with us grandkids. As my grandparents got older, smaller dogs followed: Pugs, Miniature Schnauzers, and Toy Poodles.

When my grandfather died, Grandma was alone for the first time in her life. Although some of her children and grandchildren lived nearby, she was, for the first time, the only person living in her home. However, she wasn't totally alone. There was still a Miniature Poodle named Beau. Beau had no training. In fact, he was spoiled rotten, but he kept Grandma company. He gave her a reason to go for a walk and he listened when she talked. She cooked for him, just as she had for her family. With Beau in the house, she wasn't alone.

♥　　♥　　♥

Stacy was the last of eight children. She was born deaf and her seven older brothers protected her. In doing so, they didn't allow her to meet and surmount the challenges that most children normally face. For example, she never learned to speak and was resistant to learning sign language. As a result, she was undergoing special schooling and was having trouble adjusting.

When Stacy was eight years old, she met Max, a German Shepherd Dog who had been trained just for Stacy. He alerted her to doorbells and the smoke detector, and woke her when her alarm clock went off. Most importantly, Max belonged to Stacy. He went for walks with her, slept by her bed, and ate when she fed him. She bathed him, cleaned up after him, and learned to teach him new things.

When Stacy's father saw how well she was doing with Max, he got permission from the local school district for Max to attend Stacy's classes. Within one year, Stacy was speaking understandably and was proficient in American Sign Language. When she was old enough for high school, Stacy went to a public high school without Max, who waited patiently for her at home. Ten years after getting Max, Stacy graduated with an A average from public high school and had earned several college scholarships.

Sharon, an activity director at a small residential retirement home, saw that some of the newly arrived residents were despondent and upset at having to leave their homes and a lifetime collection of belongings. She saw, too, that many of the new residents grieved for their independence, family, friends, and for the pets that could not come with them. They felt alone even though they were surrounded by people.

Using her own money, Sharon bought three parakeets and put them in cages in the rooms of the people she felt were grieving the most. She kept the residents supplied with food and other items needed to care for the birds, but allowed the residents to do the work. Within three weeks, the bird owners had become social butterflies. Other residents were stopping by the rooms to visit while the bird owners talked enthusiastically about their pets. The change was significant! The board of directors was convinced to take over the birds' expenses and to add a couple more for the recreation room.

♥   ♥   ♥

Francine moved into the retirement home when her husband passed away. Thirty-five years later, she was still there and was the unofficial historian of the facility.

"This black cat showed up on the roof outside my window about ten years ago," she said. "I watched him for a while and tried to call him. He would look at me, but wouldn't come close." After seeing him stay nearby for several days, Francine started placing food outside her window. She called the cat Stranger and has watched for him and fed him for the ensuing ten years.

"I don't know how old he is," she said. "He was an adult when he first came." She continued, "I don't know what's going to happen if he needs veterinary care, because I've never been able to touch him. I guess I'll cross that bridge when we come to it. He knows I care about him, I can hear him purr when I put out his food."

♥   ♥   ♥

The pet–people bond, and especially the dog–people bond, is strong. Dogs were probably the first domesticated animal. As dogs proved their worth as hunters, guards, and companions, they and other animals became domesticated. Time passed and the bond has grown stronger. Behaviorists, researchers, doctors, and scientists marvel at, scoff, question, and research the difference that animals make in our lives.

Why Do We Have Pets?

Most researchers agree that dogs were first domesticated because it was a mutually beneficial relationship.

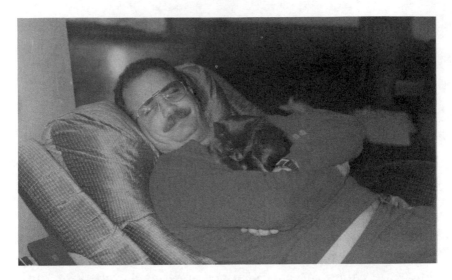

The pet–people bond is a strong one. It not only gives us a great deal of pleasure, but is good for us mentally and physically.

The early wolf-dog allowed man to share scraps of its kill or flushed game for the hunt. In return, it was allowed to seek shelter from the weather in the family cave and was given scraps from the family meal. As the wolf-dogs' value was determined, selective breeding (of a sort) was begun and domesticated dogs were born.

Today, pets serve many purposes, both as working dogs and companions. Working dogs herd sheep, protect homes and businesses, pull sleds, race, guide the blind, and help the disabled.

When allowed to do so, pet or companion dogs become more than simply a backyard resident. They, too, can work. Family dogs bark at strangers, protect against burglars, bring in the Sunday paper, and take Dad for a walk when he gets home from work. The family dog is also a confidant, listening to Junior's troubles when he has a hard day at school. The relationship between pet and owner includes physical, emotional, intellectual, and philosophical aspects, all of which have a bearing on the overall quality of life.

*Pets, and dogs in particular, provide us with
nonjudgmental, loving companionship.*

The late Dr. Boris Levinson, father of modern animal-
assisted therapy, often spoke of the pet–people bond—the
unconditional love and nonjudgmental acceptance that
dogs give to people, particularly their owners, but also to
other people. In Jacqueline P. Root's book *K-9 Therapy
Group*, Dr. Levinson had the following to say about the relationship between human and pet:

Pets are of particular help to those groups of people which our society has forced into a marginal position—children without families, the aged, the mentally retarded, the emotionally disturbed, the physically disabled and the inmates of correctional institutions. All of these people suffer from isolation, a scarcity of rewarding activities and a sense of rejection. A pet can literally mean the difference between life and death for such people.[1]

The prince and the pauper are alike in the eyes of a dog.

Dogs Provide Companionship

Today, many people are living alone. For a society that was based on a multigenerational, extended family and a strong sense of community, this is a major social change. Most people enjoy being alone occasionally, but when being alone turns into loneliness, problems arise. A person might feel cut off from the world, unwanted and unloved. At this point, a vicious circle is started: the person cannot reach out to people because he feels unworthy and, as a result, becomes more detached from the people around him.

The "Graying of America" has also influenced living habits. As the population grows older, more people are living alone after losing a spouse, as my grandmother did. The divorce rate has also created a generation of single people. A warm, loving dog can often fill the gap. The dog's unconditional love makes the person feel loved and wanted.

Pets are good for our mental health. Dr. Michael McCullough, a psychiatrist in Oregon, studied a number of physically ill patients who owned a pet. He stated that most patients felt that their pets improved their morale and gave them a feeling of support during their illness. They said that their pet distracted them from worry, made them laugh, and helped them feel needed.

[1]Jacqueline P. Root, *K-9 Therapy Group* (Fairfax, VA: Denlinger, 1990), 9.

That is part of what make Max and Stranger attractive to Stacy and Francine. Max works for Stacy as a service dog, but he also needs her for care, love, and affection. Staff members at the facility where Francine resides believe that Stranger belongs to a family near the nursing home and is cared for by them, but he spends a lot of his time on the roof near Francine's window and *she* believes that he needs her. It is such an important feeling for her that no one will change her mind.

All people have certain needs that must be met to achieve and maintain good mental health. Several researchers have conducted studies regarding these needs and have identified certain things that are important. We all need, in different ways, to be needed, to be accepted, to be trusted, and to be loved. We all need to be important to someone. Most of the time, these needs are met by other people. But the person that lives alone, or has needs that are not being met by other people, may discover that a dog really can be their best friend.

Dogs Listen

Dogs love to listen. Dog owners swear that their dog listens to every word and understands much of what is being said. It doesn't matter so much that the dog really understands. What *is* important is that the dog listens in a loving, attentive, nonjudgmental manner. Dog owners tell their dogs their deepest secrets, their dreams, their goals, their failures, and their fears. A dog never laughs or scoffs, but is simply always there—a warm, friendly presence.

Dogs Are Good for Our Physical Health

Drs. Alan Beck and Aaron Katcher reported in their book *Between Pets and People* that the presence of a pet could significantly improve physical, as well as mental and emotional, health. They found that talking to and stroking a pet reduces blood pressure and relieves stress. Dr. Erika Friedman, from the Center for Interaction of Animals and Society, studied the relationship between pet ownership and heart disease. She found that the mortality rate of patients with severe heart disease who owned pets was one-third that of patients who did not own pets.

Dogs also stimulate physical activity. Because the dog needs exercise, the owner must exercise, too. Walking, running, and throwing a ball for a dog are pleasurable activities when shared with a companion that has a wagging tail and a smiling face.

With exercise comes increased mobility, flexibility, stamina, energy, and an improved outlook on life. Throwing a ball, brushing a dog, petting a kitten, or hugging a puppy can all be unconscious forms of physical therapy. The pet stimulates the activity and the person enjoys and benefits from it.

Walking a dog not only gives the owner exercise, it is also a stimulant for social interaction. It's almost impossible to take a dog for a walk without being stopped by someone who would like to talk about him. Dogs are great ice breakers and the interactions are good for the owner's mental health.

Dogs Relieve Stress

Stress can be caused by anything that upsets us. Stress for one person might not constitute stress for another. Stress can be caused by work, relationships at work, personal relationships, traffic, financial problems, or even the weather. If stress isn't relieved, it will continue to build and grow until something gives—perhaps an emotional outburst or health problems.

Researchers know that the stresses of everyday life can harm us, physically as well as mentally. Stress reduction is especially emphasized for people with compromised immune systems. Betty Carmack, EdD, RN, Associate Professor at the University of San Francisco School of Nursing, discussed, in the January 1991 issue of *Holistic Nursing Practice*, the role of companion animals for patients with AIDS/HIV. Carmack wrote of a homebound patient who said that his cat allows him to release his stress. "If I have a hard day, I can talk to my cat and say I'm really angry." He goes on to say that he feels calmer after telling his cat about his anger and frustration.

Endocrinologist Hans Selye, in his book *The Stress of Life*, wrote that the body receives signals from the mind and responds with symptoms of stress. The result is tense muscles, headaches, upset stomach, higher blood pressure, ulcers, and increased risk of heart disease or stroke.

In her book *The Four-Footed Therapist*, Dr. Janet Ruckert writes, "Owning a pet is like living with an instant relaxation therapist." Watching, stroking, playing with, or talking to a pet has an immediate beneficial effect on the body—lowering blood pressure and relieving stress.

Dogs Make Us Laugh

Norman Cousins was the first to publicize the importance of laughter. In his book *Anatomy of an Illness as Perceived by the Patient*, he described the role of laughter in helping him reduce the amount of pain he experienced as a cancer patient. Cousins watched old Marx Brothers movies, read and listened to jokes, and basically dedicated himself to using laughter to combat the pain of his disease and the depression that threatened to accompany it. To some researchers, the amazing thing was that he succeeded.

In *Pets and Their People*, Bruce Fogle explains that nothing of importance in evolution happens without a reason. Laughter and a sense of humor are evolutionary developments. In other words, laughter and humor are there to help us survive. Fogle continues by saying that a physical and chemical basis for laughter will probably be discovered

A hug from a warm, affectionate, vibrantly
alive dog can relieve the stress of a hard day.

within the next decade, just as a chemical basis for depression was recently found.

Laughter and play go hand in hand. Dogs, cats, people, and many other animals play, especially as youngsters. Play is preparation for adulthood. Kittens play by stalking and catching anything that moves: a piece of string, paper, a blade of grass, a bug, or a shadow on the wall. This play prepares the kitten for the time when it might have to catch mice for its survival.

Play is also stimulation for laughter. Although some researchers disagree, many dog owners swear their dog has a sense of humor. For example, recently a friend and I were watching our two dogs playing with a ball. Ursa, an eight-year-old Australian Shepherd, had the ball and was dominating the game, so Missy, a four-year-old Golden Retriever, began staring into a bush. Ursa, perhaps thinking that Missy had found something even more exciting, dropped the ball and went to stand next to Missy, looking for the item at which Missy was staring. As soon as Ursa was next to her and was also looking, Missy dashed back to the ball and trotted off with it, smiling happily, her tail wagging high in the air. We were, of course, convulsed with laughter.

Laughter and play have other side effects. Communication is increased because the pet owner wants to tell his

Ursa is a natural retriever and if someone won't toss the ball for her, she will play by herself.

friends and family about the amusing things that his pet has done. As he shares the incident, he laughs again, experiencing the positive effects a second or third time. Mental stimulation results from the social interaction and also when the pet owner begins to play with the pet, trying to set up funny, amusing, or inventive games.

Play allows us to forget our adult responsibilities for a while and act like children again—running, jumping, acting silly, and interacting with our dog. Play relieves stress, is good exercise, and is good for both our mental and physical health. Most importantly, play is a wonderful time of sharing.

Dogs Provide Us with a Sense of Security

Bonnie had often wondered if her Golden Retriever, Jupiter, would protect her. He was so friendly to everyone that she was afraid he would lead a burglar to the silverware. However, Jupiter showed her how wrong she was. One night when Bonnie and Jupiter were alone, the big Golden Retriever started to growl and fuss. Thinking that the opossum in their backyard was bothering the dog, Bonnie told him to lay down and be quiet. Growling under his breath, Jupiter continued to fidget. Bonnie got up from her bed, intending to scare the opossum away so that Jupiter would go to sleep. As she stepped to her bedroom door, she saw a man looking back at her. Gasping with fright, she stepped back, allowing an enraged Jupiter to charge the intruder, who ran for the door. Bonnie and Jupiter's friends awarded him a "Hero" badge for his efforts and Bonnie never again questioned his protective ability.

Dogs Comfort with Touch

Human beings thrive on touch. A mother bonds with her baby through smell, sound, and touch. It has been speculated by the medical and psychiatric communities that people deprived of touch can die.

The person who lives alone, especially a widow or widower, often craves a loving touch. The surviving spouse misses the warm hugs, the pat on the shoulder, or the intimate cuddle that he or she shared with husband or wife. The young adult living alone misses the hugs and touches that go along with a loving family. The chronically ill also yearn for a warm, friendly touch. Unfortunately, people often stop touching someone once that person becomes ill. Whether it's a fear of contagion or of hurting the ill person, the touching stops and the patient misses it at a time when it's most important. AIDS/HIV patients, especially, mention the lack of touching due to society's perception of the disease.

The touch of a dog can be important to a person's health, both emotional and physical, especially for the chronically ill.

Touching a dog is pleasurable. The dog feels good under our hands or against our cheek. He is warm, furry, and vitally alive. We can feel his chest move in and out as he breathes, and hear his heart beat as we lay our ear against his chest.

Dogs Give Us Something to Do

Many aspects of dog ownership are beneficial to us. The dog's ability to listen without criticizing; its warm, loving touch; its need of our care—all these things are important. However, there is even more that a dog can do.

To be a good, effective, well-mannered companion, all dogs need training and all dog owners need to learn how to train their dogs effectively and humanely. In addition to teaching a dog the commands he will need to understand for day-to-day living, training teaches the dog owner patience, consistency, and the importance of a schedule and routine. A training method based on positive reinforcement and humane correction will help to develop the relationship between dog and owner.

The dog and owner that enjoy training can do a number of things together. A variety of hobbies are based on different dog activities. Dog shows, obedience trials, herding trials, and flyball competitions are all great places to meet and socialize with people sharing the same interests.

A love for dogs can also lead to volunteer work. Local humane societies and shelters depend on volunteers to help with the care of the animals, as well as to help socialize puppies, kittens, and older animals. A love for dogs can also turn into an occupation. Many veterinarians, animal health technicians, and dog groomers started in their profession because they loved dogs and other pets. The dog–owner relationship is emotional, intellectual, philosophical, and physical.

The dog–owner relationship is a love story.

Many dogs today still work for a living. One of the more traditional jobs is that of herding.

Therapy Dogs can be any breed, size, shape, or color, and any mixture of breeds. Members of the Oceanside, California, Love on a Leash therapy dog group pose with their dogs . . .

. . . and hit the open trail.

2

What Is a Therapy Dog?

In the Beginning

A therapy dog is a dog of any size, breed, color, shape, sex, or age that uses the power of the pet–people bond to help people.   The help may be emotional: by showing the person being visited that he is loved and lovable, by allowing the person to cry while hugging the dog, or by making the person laugh. The help given may be physical: by encouraging a stroke victim to move an arm to pet a dog or by encouraging someone to walk down the hall.

The first institution to use pets in a treatment program of any kind was in England. In 1792, a retreat for the mentally ill included rabbits, poultry, and pet animals as part of the living environment. Caring for these small pets was supposed to help teach the mentally ill self-control and to increase their confidence. Since records show the program lasted for a very long time, it can be assumed that it was a success.

In 1944, in the United States, the Red Cross established a rehabilitation program for disabled airmen. Each patient was matched with a dog that he then trained as part of his rehabilitation.

Following World War II, little was heard about pet or animal-assisted therapy until Dr. Boris Levinson, the "father" of pet therapy, discovered by accident the obvious benefits of using an animal to assist him in his psychiatric practice.

One day, Dr. Levinson's black Labrador Retriever, Jingles, was in the office when a client arrived—a withdrawn, very distraught young boy. The boy had a difficult time relating to Dr. Levinson, but the dog's presence helped Dr. Levinson get the boy to talk and, as a result, progress with his therapy. Jingles was not trained to work as a therapy dog. He was simply in the right place at the right time and Dr. Levinson was perceptive enough to recognize that the boy needed the dog, and that the two could work together. This recognition led to a whole new view of dogs.

The Ohio State Hospital for the Criminally Insane has the oldest pet–people program in the United States. David Lee, the resident psychologist, introduced pets to the hospital. The inmates earned the right to have a pet by convincing Lee that they were ready for the responsibility of caring for it. Each inmate had to build a cage, research the needs of the pet, and then show Lee that he was ready to care for the animal. The results of pet ownership were more drastic than even Lee had hoped. Violence in the wing where the pets were kept dropped tremendously. Suicides and tranquilizer use decreased, and communication between inmates and therapists increased.

The scientific community has recently come to realize what pet owners have always known: pets are good for us. Numerous scientific studies over the last decade show that pets in homes, institutions, schools, and prisons help people by providing companionship and love, encouraging activity, providing a listening ear, and most importantly, giving people a reason to smile.

Classifications of Therapy Dogs

"Therapy dogs" fall into two general classifications—visiting or resident and social or therapeutic. The first category differentiates between the dog's home and the second category differentiates the service the dog provides.

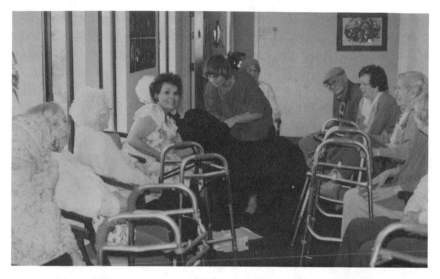

The residents of Lake Park Villas assisted-living complex look forward to their visits with the therapy dogs.

Visiting

A visiting therapy dog does just that, he visits. He is usually privately owned and visits a facility on a regular basis. The visiting therapy dog can share his love and affection with the facility's residents during each visit, but is not available after visiting hours. If a resident wishes to hug a dog at midnight when she is alone and afraid, the dog is not available. However, many visiting dogs come as part of a group, so there are more dogs, of various sizes, shapes, breeds, and colors, and there is less competition among the residents to spend time with the dog. The privately owned visiting therapy dog does not require care from the facility's staff. All care is provided by the owner.

Resident

The resident therapy dog lives in the facility and is usually available twenty-four hours a day and *will* be there to comfort someone at midnight, if needed. Rules for resident therapy dogs differ from facility to facility. Sometimes the dog is restricted to the recreation area and sometimes the dog is allowed free run of the facility. Either way, the dog is always available to the residents who enjoy his company.

The difficulty of having a resident therapy dog is that someone must be responsible for his care. The dog must be fed, exercised regularly, groomed, vaccinated, and trained. If a staff member is voluntarily willing to take on these responsibilities, there are no problems unless he or she leaves. However, if the person assigned to care for the dog is doing it grudgingly, then problems will result. Several facilities have solved the problem by having the care of the dog written into the job description and hiring a person that is not only an experienced recreation person, but also a dog owner. There must also be backup staff members able to care for the dog when the primary care person is off duty.

Social or Therapeutic

Through common usage, the term *therapy dog* has come to mean any trained, certified dog that is used to help people. However, the Delta Society, a nonprofit educational foundation that also certifies therapy dogs, clarified the terms referring to these trained dogs and classified these dogs as one of two types: animal-assisted therapy (AAT) dogs and animal-assisted activities (AAA) dogs. AAT dogs and their owners work with the patient alongside a physical therapist, a speech therapist, or other health-care professional. AAA dogs and their owners visit people and provide emotional support, but without the presence of a health-care professional.

The Foundation for Pet Provided Therapy recognizes that dogs can be of benefit in many different situations, including both social activities and different types of therapy. However, in this organization, dogs are certified in one category, as therapy dogs, rather than the two categories offered by the Delta Society.

Therapy Dog International certifies dogs only for social or activity therapy, not as therapeutic or working dogs. (For more information about certification, see Chapter 10.)

Breeds of Dogs Used

Kody Bear is a coal black, 120-pound Newfoundland with a shiny, wavy coat. His head alone is bigger than many small dogs! Yet he is a wonderful therapy dog. He is tall enough to rest his head on the rails of a bed so that bedridden patients can pet him. His silky soft coat invites a hug, and he absolutely loves children. Although he is huge, he is incredibly gentle.

Ch. Elmac's Watachie Chocho des CD, CGC, TEI is, at seven pounds, small enough to sit in laps.

Chocho, a black and white Papillon, on the other hand, weighs seven pounds. He is the perfect size to sit in a lap. During one visit, I placed him in the lap of a woman in a wheelchair. Chocho was sitting quietly while being patted. A caregiver asked me a question and I turned away. When I turned back, Chocho and the woman in the wheelchair had disappeared. A staff member motioned to me while putting her finger to her lips signaling "Be quiet." I peered around the corner where she was looking. The woman in the wheelchair was turning into her room down the hall, with Chocho still sitting in her lap. I followed them and got to her room just as she placed Chocho on her bed.

She saw me and laughed as she said, "Oh, darn! You caught us. Go away. He's going to stay here with me." Naturally, I didn't go away, but I did stay and visit with her a while.

Care Bear, the first therapy dog I trained, is an Australian Shepherd and although he was active in a variety of dog sports, including herding, agility, obedience, flyball, and schutzhund, he seemed born to be a therapy dog. He loves people intensely and is very good at sensing when someone needs him. Weighing forty-five pounds, he is tall enough that people can reach him from a chair or bed, yet small enough to cuddle should they invite him up next to them.

Kody, Care Bear, and Chocho are all effective therapy dogs, each in his own way. Dogs of any breed can be used as therapy dogs. One southern California program has German Shepherd Dogs, a Basset Hound, a Welsh Terrier, four Saint Bernards, several Australian Shepherds, Irish Setters, Border Collies, a couple of Papillons, and several mixed breeds.

Personality Plus!

The size or breed of dog isn't the most important factor in choosing a therapy dog—it's the dog's personality. A therapy dog must like people. A reticent dog might cause someone to feel that the dog doesn't want to visit with them because

Therapy dogs must obviously like people.

they aren't good enough or lovable enough. Keep in mind the people you are visiting may not always be thinking logically and are almost certainly not dog experts. This isn't a job for a shy, fearful, cautious, or retiring dog, nor is it an occupation for an aggressive one.

Therapy dogs must have a calm, stable personality that can handle and accept the unexpected. They should be bright, alert, and outgoing. Frisky dogs are okay, as long as they are not overbearing or out of control. The dogs will see, hear, and smell things to which they probably don't have access at home: hospital equipment, trays, carts, wheelchairs, walkers, canes, respiratory equipment, bandages, catheter bags, and much, much more.

A therapy dog cannot react fearfully to a cane dropping to the floor or snap at someone if a metal pan is dropped. He cannot sniff at personal things or medical equipment and ignore the person he is to visit. The dog must accept hugs patiently, even if unsteady hands pull hair or hug too tightly.

The dog must be able to handle screams, cries, or other loud vocalizations. The 23 group has visited special education classes at elementary, middle, and high schools. Children in these classes are inclined to vocalize with screams, sometimes very loudly. The dogs must be able to accept such noise without exhibiting fear, barking, growling, or pulling away.

Missy, a Golden Retriever, seemed to understand that a young teenager in the special education class was screaming because she wanted to pet a dog, whereas some people in the classroom thought that the girl was afraid. Missy knew better and, ignoring the volume of the girl's screams, went directly to her. When the girl's hand was guided to Missy's head, the vocalizations immediately quieted and the screams were replaced with giggles.

The dog must show by facial expressions and body language that he likes people. If a dog is too reserved, people will sense this and be less apt to want to pet him. Care Bear exhibits good body language. He greets people and then turns and sits next to a chair or wheelchair so that the person's hand falls to his head. If they do not start petting immediately, he moves closer and nudges their hand with his nose, urging them to pet him. His visits have caused many people to smile, simply because he leaves no doubt in anyone's mind exactly what they are supposed to do!

Age and Sex

Although everyone loves a warm, fuzzy puppy, their visits are severely restricted. Puppies can be easily frightened, with repercussions that could last throughout their life. Puppies may not be fully house-trained and may not have all of their immunizations. Puppies should visit only one or two people at a time, for no more than ten to fifteen minutes total. The puppy should, however, be started in a puppy kindergarten class, where he will be introduced to basic commands and socialized with other people and puppies.

After four months of age, a puppy's training can be started in earnest and the visits can be slowly increased in duration, depending on the puppy's progress. Be careful that the puppy regards the visits as fun instead of serious work.

It is not necessary for a therapy dog to start as a puppy. Some of the most successful therapy dogs I know started as adults. Care Bear, mentioned earlier, was four years old when he started therapy work. Shawna, a Golden Retriever, started at age twelve and loves it! Her whole attitude says, "Yes! I've been waiting my whole life to do this!"

The sex of the dog is not important, either. Both males and females can be therapy dogs; however, most experts recommend that the dogs be spayed or neutered. There are several reasons for this. First, a good therapy dog simply does not need the sexual hormones. The bitch will not come into season after she has been spayed; that alone gives her a more dependable working life. The neutered male is less apt to lift his leg and mark territory, and will be less apt to fight with the other male dogs. Both males and females are thought to have a decreased risk of cancer as they get older after early neutering, giving them a longer working life. And last, the pet overpopulation problem decrees that most dogs should be spayed or neutered.

Training Is Required

Therapy dogs are required to be very well trained. The dogs cannot jump on people, paw, or scratch. They cannot use their mouths—no biting, mouthing, or licking. Some

Shawna, a Golden Retriever, was twelve years old when she started therapy work. She loves it and the senior citizens she visits empathize with her white hair and stiff joints.

therapy dog owners teach their dog to lick (or "kiss") on command and this is acceptable as long as the dog learns to kiss a cheek (only on command) and not the person's mouth. Therapy dogs must be under their owner's complete control, with no wild leaping, pulling, or barking allowed.

Grooming

Therapy dogs must be clean, neat, and parasite free when they visit, and they should have a bath the day of or the day before a visit. Dogs need not be in the same coat condition or cut that they would need for conformation showing. For example, a Poodle or a Shih Tzu can be in a short clip. What is most important is that the dog is clean and appears well cared for and healthy.

The dogs cannot have fleas, ticks, or mites. It is vitally important for the health of the dog and of the people you are visiting that the dog is parasite free.

The dog should have his nails trimmed regularly, ideally several days before a visit, because freshly trimmed nails can be very sharp. Cleaning the ears should be a regular part of the grooming routine, as should checking the anal glands. If you have any questions about what you need to do to keep your dog properly groomed, make an appointment with a groomer in your area. Pay her for her time, but ask her to show you how to trim your dog's nails, to trim the hair between his pads, to check his anal glands, and to clean his ears. Ask what kind of a brush you should use for his coat type. She will be glad to help you.

Health Requirements

Therapy dogs must be healthy. They cannot be coughing, sneezing, vomiting, or show any other sign of illness. There are other less-obvious health matters that are important to you, the dog, and his ability to work well, and to the people that you are visiting.

Your dog should have a fecal flotation or exam by your veterinarian to check for internal parasites. After receiving an "all clear" the dog should be rechecked regularly, depending on your veterinarian's recommendation. In some areas, especially those areas in which there is no winter freeze, the dog might need to be rechecked every four months. Other dogs in other locations may need a six-month recheck. When you talk to your vet, ask him to describe the symptoms of parasite infestation so that you can watch for them in between rechecks. Regardless of the schedule you keep, the dog must be free of internal parasites when you visit.

All dogs must be up-to-date on all recommended vacci-nations. Most areas require a distemper combination vac-cine, which may or may not include parvo and parain-fluenza. If it does not, those should be administered separately. The dog should also have corona, bordatella, and rabies vaccinations. Some areas also require or recom-mend other vaccines. Again, check with your veterinarian.

A Therapy Dog at Last

A dog is not a therapy dog until it has satisfied all the requirements for certification. Certification requires train-ing, socializing, passing an evaluation, demonstrating the ability to do the work, and more. Chapter 10, How Do You and Your Dog Become Certified?, explains these proce-dures.

3

Who Benefits from Therapy Dogs?

All of the benefits of pet ownership discussed so far can apply to a therapy dog, plus many, many more. A warm, friendly, nonjudgmental, caring animal that is also incredibly well trained makes for a superb motivator. The dog can be important to the individual, of course, but can also be of use to the caretakers, the physical therapists, the staff psychologist, the activities director, and everyone else on the staff at nursing homes, hospitals, day-care centers, and special schools.

Individuals Benefit

The Love on a Leash visiting therapy dog group was spread out throughout one of the nursing homes that the group regularly visits. Each dog's partner knocked on a resident's door and asked if he or she would like to visit with a dog. In one room, Kody, a Newfoundland, had his head resting on the bed next to a frail, elderly gentleman named Charles. Charles had always been enthusiastic about the dogs and during each visit to the facility, the dogs' partners made sure that he got a chance to pet the dogs.

This time, however, one of Charles' daughters was also visiting her Dad and a few minutes into the visit she became very agitated and asked the dog's partner to step into the hallway.

"Dad was talking to you," she said.

Therapy dogs make people smile. When people smile, their entire day is brightened. They feel better about themselves and the world in general. Here, Trouper (Bellvue's Broadway Trouper, CD, HC, TT, TDI, VC) greets a friend, Mae, at the Alzheimer's Family Center. Trouper is owned by Janet and Rick Wall. Photo by Janet Wall.

Joan Swanson, Kody's owner and partner replied, "Yes, he always talks to us. He always remembers our dogs' names and he's told us about dogs he used to have. He's always been very friendly."

"No, you don't understand," she said. "Dad hasn't spoken to any family members or caretakers for more than five years."

Why did Charles talk to the dogs and their partners and not to his family or caretakers? It's hard to tell. Perhaps it was because the dogs placed no demands on him. If he wanted to be quiet and simply stroke the dog's head, that was fine. However, if he wanted to share his memories of dogs long gone, that was okay too. One of his caretakers said that Charles smiled only when the dogs were with him. Another staff member said that he was angry with his family for admitting him to the nursing home. When asked why he didn't speak to his family, Charles said simply, "I didn't have anything to say."

Pets are good for our emotional health. Although we really don't know scientifically how they affect us, we do know that the visiting dogs stimulate Charles so that he opens up, talks, and smiles. Innumerable other nursing home residents have reacted in a similar fashion. Residents that rarely request to get up ask staff members to dress them and comb their hair so that they look presentable "for the dogs."

At day-care centers and schools, children can pet the therapy animals when they come to visit and those that do not live with pets get a chance to meet a dog or other pet. The well-trained dogs can stimulate intellectual growth by triggering curiosity. Why does the dog wear a collar? Why does he jump over the jump? How do you teach him?

Nonthreatening, gentle dogs also help children overcome fear. Kathy was four years old when a group of visiting therapy dogs came to her day-care center. She had been badly frightened by a dog when she was younger and her parents had signed the permission slip for her to see

This Sheltie works well with tots. Photo from the Weldon albums.

the dogs, but warned the caretakers that she was afraid. One of the teachers kept Kathy off to the side so that she could see the action, but wouldn't feel threatened. First the dogs did a little show, doing some obedience work, demonstrating some tricks, and catching Frisbees. Kathy was watching Chocho, a Papillon. At seven pounds, Chocho was by far the smallest dog visiting. Kathy's teacher noticed her interest and waved for Chocho's partner to bring him over. After some initial hesitation, Kathy reached out to touch him. "Oh! He's so soft!" she said. In response, Chocho nosed her hand. Her teacher told her, "He wants you to pet him some more." In the space of seconds, a fear was faced and a friendship born.

The mental stimulation of a visiting dog can cause a chain reaction. The resident has a good time during the visit, laughs, talks with other residents, talks with staff members, and, in general, enjoys himself. After a visit, the activities director or teacher can use the mental stimulation by having the residents draw pictures of the dogs and what they did, or write thank you notes to the dogs' partners. Disabled children can draw or talk about the visit. This causes a sense of excitement and anticipation for the next visit.

Groups Benefit

Pets are wonderful creatures for breaking down social barriers. Many dog owners have recognized that it's almost impossible to take their dog for a walk without being stopped by someone to talk about dogs. Therapy dogs cause even more of the same reaction. Both visiting and resident therapy dogs can break down barriers that people build around themselves. People from dramatically different cultures and lifestyles can all talk about dogs: their own, other people's, and the visiting dogs. The common experiences allow people to initiate conversations, share memories, laugh, and sometimes cry.

The visiting pets often spark a spirit of cooperation among residents. When the day for a visit arrives, a couple of people can watch for the dogs' arrival and notify the rest of the group, "The dogs are here!" Gloria Francis, PhD, FAAN, found that in a visiting puppy program through her local Society for the Prevention of Cruelty to Animals (SPCA), the nursing home residents began anticipating the puppies' arrival, would notify each other throughout the facility, and, in general, cooperated as a group much more than they had ever done in other situations.

"Puppy power" significantly improved the quality of life at the nursing home. Francis' article, "Here Come the Puppies," described her study, which tested the hypothesis that

Dogs have an appeal to people of all ages and
many dog owners have found that it's
impossible to go for a walk without
talking to people about your dog.

weekly domestic animal visitations to people residing in a nursing home increases the quality of life in several ways: life satisfaction, psychological well-being, social competence, social interest, and a number of other factors. At the end of the eight-week study, Francis found that the puppies worked magic. The majority of the indicators being tested improved significantly.

We need to be needed and nothing needs us quite as much as
a young, fuzzy, affectionate puppy.

The Staff Benefits

Visiting or resident therapy dogs build morale for the
staff almost as much as for the residents. When the dogs do
tricks or perform a show, the staff is usually encouraged to
attend. Then, while the dogs visit with individual residents,
many staff members watch, take notes, and share the joys
and sorrows. Vicariously, they experience the benefits of pet
ownership and work-related stress, which is frequently high

in these professions, is relieved. After all, staff members, too, need a nonjudgmental, friendly cuddle from a happy dog or a purring cat.

The presence of pets helps deinstitutionalize a facility. This more homelike setting can improve the residents' psychological well-being, as well as the staff's morale. A couple of parakeets, caged in different wings of the facility, will sing throughout the day, their happy chirping spreading cheer. A cat, jumping from bed to bed or from lap to lap, becomes a magnet for smiles. A dog's wagging tail and happy face invites a pat.

Often, a therapy dog assists the staff's professional efforts. An anticipated visit is used to motivate a resident to get out of bed, shower, dress, and socialize with other people. Once a resident begins talking about a visiting pet, the caretaker can lead the conversation in many directions and gain information she might not be able to obtain in other situations.

Physical therapists use therapy dogs with much success. Residents are much more eager to go for their daily walk if the dog can walk with them. The dogs are taught to move slowly and not to pull, and can walk beside a walker or a wheelchair. Brushing the dog requires arm and shoulder movements, balance, and hand coordination. Checking a dog's paw for cuts or scratches requires fine finger motions, as does hooking or unhooking a leash. Sometimes any hand or arm movement is therapeutic: stroking or petting the dog, shaking hands, rubbing the dog's tummy, or combing or holding a pet.

Different specialists use the dogs to their own advantage. Activity directors normally schedule therapy dog visits as part of regular activities. If other specialists coordinate with the activity director, individual goals can be pursued. Psychologists, occupational therapists, recreation therapists, physical therapists, nurses, and doctors can all be involved. A little ingenuity and planning are all it takes.

The Resident's Family Benefits

Guilt is a common emotion for families of nursing home residents. In most instances, the son, daughter, or spouse would rather have the family member at home, but simply cannot provide the necessary care. When a therapy dog program is in effect, the family members become more comfortable with the nursing home and with the care that their loved one is receiving.

At many facilities, families are invited to visit when the therapy dogs are working. Many are overwhelmed by the residents' responses to the pets.

Arthur, a retired Navy admiral, and a handsome, polite gentleman, resided in an Alzheimer's facility. The therapy dogs had been visiting him for several months. One day while the dogs were visiting, Arthur's son came to pick him up for lunch. After watching his dad and a dog for about a half an hour, he told the group, "Dad was more lucid today . . . while talking to you and petting the dogs than I have seen him in years. Thank you very much." In the following weeks, Arthur's son often dropped in during the therapy dog visits and even brought his video camera to record the event for the rest of the family.

Therapy dog groups are encouraged to visit during family support group meetings. There, family members can be told exactly what the dogs do, and how dogs are screened, trained, and handled. Misconceptions, concerns, or fears can be addressed. The family members should meet some of the dogs and get a chance to see them work. Reading materials can be distributed to those wanting to know more about the field.

The Therapy Dog's Owner Benefits

My grandparents played an important part during my childhood. I remember spending weekends in their old house, away from my parents and siblings, just me and Grandma and Grandpa. I loved to explore their attic, finding old dresses, pictures, and other memorabilia. I would raid the cookie jar, thinking that I was getting away with something, but I now know that I really wasn't. Grandpa introduced me to fishing. I liked the sitting around and relaxing part, hated the worm and fish part, but I went along with it because I was spending time with him. All in all, I have wonderful memories of my grandparents.

They were lucky. They were both able to grow old in their own home, surrounded by family and dogs. Now that I have been visiting nursing homes with therapy dogs for a number of years, I realize that one of the primary reasons that I do this is because of my grandparents. They gave me so much love and laughter. I want to share that wonderful part of my life with people that might not otherwise have it. The people that I am visiting are not able to live at home and many do not have family nearby. I can give them a hug, show them that I care, bring them a Valentine or a candy cane, and share my dogs with them.

Other therapy dog partners are attracted for different reasons. One man's mother passed away in a nursing home and he found it hard to let go of the guilt, feeling that if he had taken care of her at home she wouldn't have died. It was an illogical thought, but knowing that didn't exorcise it. So he began visiting to cure himself of his fear of nursing homes. As he came to know the residents, he began to enjoy the visits and was able to rid himself of his guilt. A nurse visits because she likes people and a young woman visits because she loves her dog and just wants to share her with others not so fortunate. The reasons for getting involved as a therapy dog partner are as varied as the dogs and the people that own them.

Although the rewards are tremendous, all therapy dog partners agree that it can be very difficult at times, especially when someone of whom you have grown fond becomes ill or passes away. A smile, a happy tear, a hug, or a spoken word from someone who never talks is worth all the time, effort, and occasional disappointments.

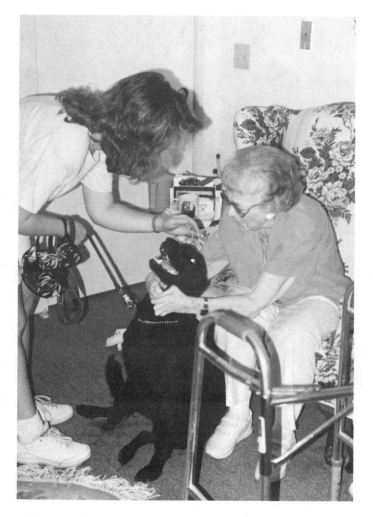

Therapy dog partners get as much enjoyment from their visits as the people they are visiting.

*Thousands of years of evolution have produced dogs
with a wide variety of physical characteristics.
Zippy, a Welsh Terrier, and Gracie, a Basset Hound,
are both therapy dogs registered with the
Foundation for Pet Provided Therapy.*

4

Can Your Dog Be a Therapy Dog?

Does Your Dog Have These Qualities?

When evaluating any dog—no matter whether he is a pet, companion, obedience competition dog, conformation show dog, or working dog—for possible work as a therapy dog, the dog's personality and temperament are of the utmost importance. Just as with people, individual dogs have different personalities and temperaments. Dogs of the same breed, even from the same litter, can be totally different.

It's important that generalizations are not made regarding potential therapy dogs. All Australian Shepherds are not good therapy dogs, even though many Australian Shepherds are serving in this role wonderfully. Just because some Rottweilers can be aggressive does not mean that others do not make good therapy dogs. Many Rottweilers are kind, caring, well-behaved therapy dogs. Each dog must be evaluated individually.

The ideal therapy dog should be alert and attentive to what is happening around him, but focused enough to remember what he's supposed to be doing. A dog that is too distracted may not be able to concentrate. He should be happy to be around people and should demonstrate this with a wiggling body, wagging tail, or smiling face.

A potential therapy dog must be even tempered, good-natured, and able to accept handling by other people

41

without growling, snapping, or raising a fuss. Very few people will be intentionally rough with therapy dogs, but sometimes hands crippled by disease or a lifetime of overwork are rough and the dog must be able to take the handling.

A therapy dog cannot be aggressive toward people or the other dogs participating in the program. He cannot react to anything by growling, snapping, or biting. The dog should not be overly submissive, either. Submissive urination (when the dog is touched or picked up) is not allowed.

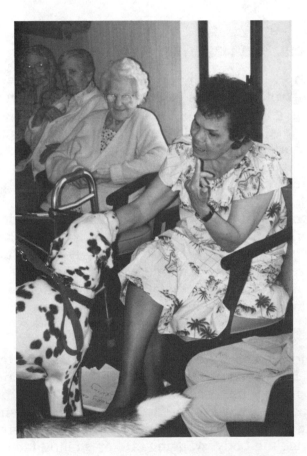

A potential therapy dog must be even tempered, outgoing, and very people oriented.

Is Your Dog Good with Adults and Children?

It's important that a therapy dog be well socialized with people. A dog that grows up in a household with lots of people is a potentially better candidate than a dog that has been isolated in the backyard. Socialization with people of all sizes, shapes, sex, and ethnic heritage is very important. The dog that grows up never seeing children may think that children are strange creatures from another planet. Children move more quickly and less smoothly than adults. To a dog, children are not simply small people, but something quite different.

Children and dogs should always be supervised, but together they can teach each other and form wonderful friendships.

Although the most important time to socialize a dog is during puppyhood, when he is forming his attachments to people, socialization is an ongoing process. The dog should routinely be taken different places: the shopping center, the lumber yard, the park, and the beach. He must learn that people like him, want to pet him, and are, in general, friendly.

Early socialization helps puppies bond with people.

The southern California chapter of the Love on a Leash Therapy Dog Program routinely schedules socialization outings. The group will meet at a local shopping center or other public place and spend one and one-half hours walking the dogs, visiting with people, and practicing obedience commands in public. The dogs learn to behave in very distracting circumstances and, at the same time, meet a variety of people. As a side benefit, people see the dogs, ask what they are and what they do, and the group gets some additional publicity and occasionally recruits a new member or two.

A visit to the local mall is a great place to socialize with people of all ages, sizes, and varieties; and, as a side benefit, allows the dog to get comfortable walking on slick floors.

If the dog shows a dislike or fear of a particular person, he should never be forced up to that person. He is not, however, allowed to dash or pull away. When the dog's partner senses the dog's fear, the dog is asked to sit and hold his position. Force him to concentrate on holding still instead of concentrating on the person of whom he is afraid. This way, the fear is faced, but not reinforced, and he can be praised for his obedience.

Zippy, a Welsh Terrier, was afraid of children as a puppy. One day, Zippy and her owner started to walk past a school where the kids had just returned after summer vacation. Zippy was used to the school yard being empty—finding it full of running, playing, screaming children was too much. Zippy pulled back on the leash, fighting to run away from the kids. Her owner, of course, wanted Zippy to overcome this fear, so she planned a systematic program of desensitizing Zippy to the children. Each day, she would walk Zippy toward the school. When Zippy started to show fear, she would take three more steps into the "fear zone," then stop and tell Zippy to sit and stay. Zippy was required to hold the stay and sit, facing the kids. After a few seconds, Zippy was praised for sitting and allowed to walk away.

Very gradually, the fear zone shrunk, allowing Zippy to get closer and closer to the children. When Zippy was confident enough for children to approach her, her owner controlled the petting sessions so that each child approached slowly and asked for permission before touching Zippy. If Zippy appeared nervous, she was turned around so that the kids patted her back instead of her head. Over a period of months Zippy learned that the children wouldn't hurt her and that she got lots of praise and petting for interacting with them. Although she may never be totally comfortable with children, she now understands that they can touch her without hurting her.

Even though Zippy doesn't live with children and could have gone through life without interacting with them, her owner wasn't willing to accept this fear or the risk of Zippy some day biting a child. "I didn't want Zip to try to run away or climb up my leg every time she saw a child," her owner said. "I wanted to be able to take her places where there might be children, such as the store or the nursing home, and have her behave reliably and the without fear."

Is Your Dog Body Sensitive?

Does your dog cry every time he gets a vaccination or is he the stoic kind? Body sensitivity can be seen in several forms, one of which is the dog's pain threshold. Dogs that have a low pain tolerance, those that cry at the slightest hurt, will react to touch very differently than the dog with a high pain threshold.

A therapy dog must enjoy being touched. He cannot be so body sensitive that petting causes fear or hyperactivity.

Ursa, one of my Australian Shepherds, is not very body sensitive. To pet her so that she enjoys it, I thump on her rib cage and scratch (hard) down her back. Because of this, Ursa is a good therapy dog to use in situations when the person she is visiting might be rough.

On the other hand, some dogs are upset by rough handling. Gretchen, a lovely Doberman Pinscher, cries when she gets her vaccinations or when her owner uses the training collar to correct misbehavior. Because she is very body sensitive, Gretchen is best used when visiting quiet, gentle people.

Is Your Dog Hand Shy?

Hand shyness is when a dog ducks away from an outstretched hand, even if no threatening gesture has been made. This reaction on the dog's part can cause people to feel the dog doesn't like them or is afraid of them.

Hand shyness can be caused by slapping or hitting a dog as a means of discipline. A dog should *never* be hit or slapped. This is rarely an effective means of training.

To overcome hand shyness, offer the dog an irresistible treat, approaching the dog from the front. Place your hand with the treat lower than the dog's head. When the dog takes the treat, gently scratch the dog's chin while praising him. Moving slowly, scratch the dog's ears and rub the top of his head. If the dog starts to duck away, stop petting the top of his head and go back to scratching his chin. Depending on the extent of the problem, it may take a while before the dog stops ducking his head and pulling away at quick hand movements.

Is Your Dog Good Around Other Dogs?

Most visiting therapy dogs go in a group and all of the dogs need to get along with each other. There can be no growling, dominance posturing, fighting, barking, or other disruptive behavior. Even residential dogs must be good with other dogs, as visitors will come in occasionally, bringing a visiting therapy dog or a family pet.

Visiting therapy dogs usually travel as a group. Therefore, they must be reliable and nonaggressive toward other dogs.

Does Your Dog Like Obedience Training?

Every potential therapy dog must have some basic obedience training. If the dog is accepted into a therapy dog program, additional specialized training is required. Some dogs, by temperament and personality, accept training easier than others. Also, some breeds were bred to respond better to training. For example, sighthounds were bred to chase down game using their excellent vision. The northern breeds were designed to run all day in the cold and snow, pulling a sled. Herding dogs were bred to herd sheep, ducks, and cattle.

A breed that was designed to work and take direction must be able to accept training. A breed that was bred to rely on instinct, such as a Terrier catching a rat, does not need to take direction from its owner. Genetic heritage has quite a lot of bearing on how a dog responds to training. However, this does not mean that a Terrier is good for nothing but catching rats. Terriers are very trainable, as are all other breeds.

Some working-dog schools (guide dogs, hearing dogs, narcotic or law enforcement dogs) use the dog's retrieving instincts to test potential working-dog puppies. When the pup is eight weeks old, a piece of crumpled paper is tossed about four feet away, in front of the puppy. If the puppy runs after it, picks it up, and brings it back, he is showing strong retrieving instincts and will be kept in the training program. If he runs out and brings the paper partway back, he may be evaluated further. But if the pup goes out to the paper, runs past it, or does not go after it at all, he is not considered for inclusion in the program. Some schools believe in this test so strongly that if the puppy does not show good retrieving instincts, it is not accepted into the program no matter how good he tests in other areas.

Obviously, there is more to training than just genetics and retrieving. Training is much easier if the dog cooperates willingly with the training process. If he is resistant to training, the chances of him succeeding in a therapy dog program are greatly decreased. A training program that uses positive reinforcement is much more apt to make the dog cooperate with the training. Also, positive reinforcement (praise, petting, toys, and food treats) can be used in public and in institutions where the therapy dog visits, whereas harsh corrections should not be made as they are apt to distress the people you are visiting.

Is Your Dog Reliable with Distractions?

Reliability covers several different factors. A therapy dog must demonstrate that he will react in a predictable manner to different distractions. If a metal dish or pan is

A therapy dog does not have to be a competition obedience dog,
but he does need to demonstrate a willingness to learn and
the ability to apply what he has learned.

dropped to the floor, will he flinch and look at the pan? A
reaction is to be expected. After all, you will probably react,
too, by flinching and turning around to look. Ideally, the
dog will turn to look at the sound and then will go back to
work. However, the dog should not try to pull the leash
from your hand and run away. Nor should the dog urinate
in fear at the sound or snap and growl.

It's important that the dog's owner or partner under-
stand how the dog will react in different circumstances.
These situations should be set up during the training or
evaluation process, prior to the dog ever entering a nursing
home or school. Drop a pan or tip a wheelchair on its side.
Expose the dog to a hissing air tube and a vacuum cleaner.
The dog should react in a curious but controlled manner.
He should not react fearfully, or try to snap or bite.

*Rich drops a wheelchair on its side to test Misty's
sensitivity to sounds. As a therapy dog, she must
accept these types of sounds without fear.*

He must also be reliable in his interactions with people. If the dog is frightened of certain people, as Zippy was of children, the fear must be overcome prior to the dog becoming involved in the therapy dog program.

Is Your Dog House-Trained?

A good therapy dog needs to be completely and reliably house-trained. There should never be any "accidents" while visiting. You also need to know your dog's body language so that if he needs to relieve himself, you can take him outside to an appropriate area. You must *always* carry a plastic bag to clean up after your dog.

Is Your Dog Healthy?

A good therapy dog must be healthy, but there are exceptions that can actually make the therapy dog more effective. An older dog that may be arthritic or have a cataract can be a very effective therapy dog, as long as he is otherwise healthy and in no pain. The senior citizens that you visit in the nursing home may bond more rapidly to a white-faced, gray-muzzled old dog than a frisky, energetic puppy.

A dog that has lost a leg in an accident or to cancer can be very appealing to people facing the same problems. Misty is a black Labrador Retriever that has a deformed front leg as a result of a birth defect. She is very appealing to many people, who see her as a source of strength, because she is coping well with her deformity. She runs and plays and keeps up with the other dogs who have four strong legs. She is a wonderful motivator for people undergoing physical therapy.

If you are in doubt about your dog's ability to participate in a therapy dog program because of a physical problem, talk to your veterinarian. Is this problem a danger to people with a compromised immune system? Could this problem get worse if the dog participates?

If you get an "Okay, do it" from your veterinarian, then think carefully about how you can explain the health problem to the people you are visiting. The explanation should be short, upbeat, and in layman's terms. "Misty's leg was deformed when she was born, but it doesn't hurt her and she has learned to make allowances for it." Or, "Thumper's eye was injured when he was a puppy, but he sees very well with his other eye." Emphasize that the dog is not in any discomfort and don't go into long drawn-out explanations that might confuse the person to whom you're talking.

Do You Have the Time to Groom Your Dog Regularly?

When choosing or evaluating a potential therapy dog, the amount of time and effort needed to keep up the dog's coat needs to be taken into consideration. The dog needs to be freshly groomed before each visit. This means bathed, dried, brushed, and, if necessary, trimmed.

Jeri Klosson Todd has two Standard Poodles and one Toy Poodle, all therapy dogs. If she decides to bring all three dogs on a visit, that means that she will need to spend a good part of the day before the visit grooming dogs—a big investment of time and energy.

Mischka is a Siberian Husky. She is a very affectionate therapy dog, but can only participate during part of the year because she has a very dense, thick undercoat that she sheds twice a year. Although her owner would like to participate more often, it is very unfair for her to go to a facility and leave white hairs on everything. The housekeeping staff should not have to work harder because the dogs come to visit.

5

What Basic Training Does a Therapy Dog Need?

Your ability to communicate affects how a dog learns. A dog will do anything to please us, so it's up to us to figure out how to tell him what we want him to do. If we can't give a command properly, we can't expect the dog to learn it.

Training Methods

There are many dog-training techniques used by professional trainers. I advocate what I find most successful—positive reinforcement with an appropriately timed correction.

Positive Reinforcement

When training a dog, use as much positive reinforcement as possible, *because it works.* Positive reinforcement tells a dog that what he did was good and encourages him when he's unsure. The positive reinforcements used will vary from dog to dog, depending on the dog's response. The most common reinforcements include verbal praise, petting, food treats, and toys.

Verbal praise should be given in a high-pitched, happy voice. Please don't scream at your dog, however. Simply use a joyful tone. The amount of verbal praise depends on the individual dog and the situation. A good sit might be rewarded with, "Good boy!" However, if you and your dog have been working on a difficult exercise and he suddenly makes a breakthrough, and performs the exercise successfully, then reward him with more extravagant praise: "Thank you! What a good boy! Super!"

Dreamcycle, like most dogs, works eagerly for positive reinforcement, especially praise and treats.

The timing of verbal praise is critical. When you command your dog to sit, you should praise him as soon as his rump hits the ground. If you delay the praise, he might think he's being praised for holding still, instead of sitting on command. Later, when you are working with exercises your dog already knows, the praise can be given at the end of an exercise. Even then, if the dog tries extra hard or does something very well, praise him during the exercise.

The petting or physical praise that you give to reinforce your dog's actions positively include ear scratches, chest rubs, hugs, or anything else that gives both you and your dog pleasure. If your dog is very body sensitive, then physical praise should be limited to the amount that he can tolerate without getting overstimulated—maybe just a scratch behind the ear.

Physical praise should always be accompanied by verbal praise. Your voice is your most important training tool. During training there will be many times when you will only use your voice to praise him and that may be the only positive reinforcement for that moment. However, all other positive reinforcements should never be given alone; they are always accompanied by verbal praise.

Food is another positive reinforcement and is the easiest way to capture a dog's attention. Use food during training in two different ways: as a lure and as a reward. For example, teach a dog to lay down on command using the treat as an incentive. Hold the treat in your right hand. Let the dog see and smell the treat. As you give the down command, move your hand that is holding the treat to the floor right in front of the dog's paws so that he follows the treat and lays down. You are using the treat as a training tool, just like a leash.

When the dog lays down, praise him, and give him the treat. Now the treat becomes part of your positive reinforcement, a motivator. Again, just like petting, food treats should always be accompanied by verbal praise. As the dog becomes proficient in an exercise, decrease the number and frequency of treats. Use them randomly, but give verbal praise all the time.

The food treat that you use depends on your dog's taste. A tiny piece of dog beef jerky is good, or a bit of hot dog, or a piece of cheese. Whatever you use should be small and easily and quickly eaten by the dog without much chewing. You don't want the dog to get full, you just want to tempt him.

Kathy helps her puppy learn something new by talking to the pup in an upbeat, happy tone of voice, by using food treats to show the pup what she wants him to do, and by rewarding him with the treat. Most importantly, she is patient and helps her dog learn a little bit at a time.

There are some dogs that will not or cannot work for food treats. If the dog doesn't regard food as a reward, then the treat is not going to be a good motivator. If the dog is on a strict diet, food treats will only add calories. For these dogs, some other incentive (or motivator) is needed. How about a tennis ball? Or a racket ball for a smaller dog? Or a Frisbee? A foxtail toy? A squeaky toy? You need to use something that the dog loves to motivate him. Use the motivator, whatever it may be, as a lure and reward during training sessions.

Corrections

A correction is used to stop unwanted behavior. If your dog is misbehaving during a nursing home visit, a verbal "Acck! That's enough!" will interrupt the behavior and let your dog know that he made a mistake. However, the correction itself isn't as crucial as what you do after stopping the behavior. If the dog was barking, praise him for being quiet. If he was stealing something, praise him for dropping it. Reward the desired behavior.

Verbal corrections should be given in a firm, authoritative tone. Don't scream, yell, or lose your temper. Each correction should get your dog's attention immediately.

For Topo, a Toy Poodle, a stern look and a quiet verbal correction are enough to stop unwanted behavior.

Just as with positive reinforcement, the timing of corrections is very important. A correction will not work to interrupt the unwanted behavior if the dog has already stopped prior to you giving the correction. Interrupt and correct the unwanted behavior *as it is happening.*

Training Tips

Set your dog up for success, not failure. To do this, each time you teach him something new, break up the exercise into small steps and teach each step thoroughly before going on to the next. *Work on only one behavior at a time.* In this way, your dog has lots of successes, not one big failure.

Praise your dog every time he does something correctly. Don't make him feel bad about making a mistake. Correct him for the mistake, help him do what you want, and then praise him.

Don't skip training steps. Teach each exercise a step at a time. If your dog has trouble with a new step, go back a step or two and review what he's already learned. It might be clearer to him a second time through. If he still doesn't understand, look at what he's doing wrong. Where is the misunderstanding? Are you giving conflicting commands? Analyze how *you* are communicating.

Always train positively. If your dog has hit the proverbial wall and is having trouble understanding something, go back a training step or two and end your training session on a positive note. Then, at your next training session, start a couple of steps back from where he was having trouble and work back up. Sometimes having a day off from training that particular exercise allows your dog to assimilate the new information.

Teaching the Six Basic Commands

Six basic commands are the foundation necessary for therapy dogs. Those commands are release, sit, down, stay, walk on leash, and come. These exercises can be taught to puppies, young dogs, and even older dogs. The key to making them work for you is to follow the training steps as they are given here. Don't be in a hurry and skip steps. Training requires patience, persistence, consistency, and repetition.

Teaching the Release

During much of his training, you will be asking your dog to control his own actions and in many cases this will be very difficult. To help ease his stress during both training and working, you will use the release command and allow him to hop around, stretch, play, and just act like a regular dog.

To teach him the release command, use the word "Release!" with verbal praise and the dog's motivator (e.g., a toy, a favorite game). At the end of each training exercise, say, "Release!" to your dog, then praise him and encourage him to hop around. Give him his treat or toy and play with him.

During the release, the dog should be given a toy or treat that he likes. Allow him to play and lessen the stress of training.

When he has completed his training and is working as a therapy dog, the release allows him to move about, stretch, and forget about the job that he's been doing. As a side benefit, these releases can help you, too. While your dog is relaxing, you can review the next training steps, think about the next nursing home resident to visit, or join your dog in some well-deserved relaxation.

Teaching the Sit

The sit is a very simple but important command. Your dog needs to learn to sit for a treat, his meals, his toys, and, most importantly for a therapy dog, he must sit while he is being petted. He is not allowed to jump on people to be petted.

The sit means that the dog's rear end should be on the ground, his front legs should be planted squarely, and he should not move from this position. Use your hands to help place your dog in the sit position while you teach him the command. Precede each command with your dog's name. To demonstrate, we'll use the name "Jake." The exercise is taught using a progression of steps. Repeat each step several times and proceed to the next level only after your dog has mastered each step.

1. With your dog leashed and standing at your left side, gather up the excess leash in your right hand. As you give him the command, "Jake, Sit!" use your right hand and take hold of the front of his collar and push slightly up and back as you slide your left hand down his back, around his hips, and tuck his back legs under him. Keep your right hand on the collar under his chin, pet him with your left hand as you praise him, "Good boy to sit!" If he tries to pop back up, correct him, "Acck!" reposition him in the sit (using the command again), then praise him again when he's sitting.

2. Give the sit command. Hold the collar with your right hand, slide your left hand down the dog's back, *but don't tuck his back legs under him.* Continue to keep your right hand on his collar, pet with your left hand after he sits, and praise him.

3. Give the sit command. Hold the dog's collar in front with your right hand, but *keep your left hand off the dog while he sits.* Pet him with your left hand after he sits, and praise him.

4. Give the sit command. *Hold the leash close in your right hand, but do not touch his collar.* Again, keep your left hand off the dog while he executes the sit. Pet and praise him after he sits. Don't be in a hurry to get your hand off of your dog's collar. If he's antsy and is trying to get up from the sit, keep your hand on his collar and don't move on to the next step until he is ready. It is not a failure to go back and repeat steps. It's a smart trainer who recognizes when her dog needs extra work and waits until her dog is ready to move on.

5. Give the sit command, *with both hands off the dog, from a position about two steps away from your dog.* Pet and praise him after he sits.

6 With your dog in a sit by your side, *have someone walk up to you both and attempt to pet him.* If he gets up or tries to jump up, interrupt him with your voice ("Acck! No jump!") and reposition him in the sit. Don't let anyone pet him until he's sitting. Continue practicing until he will hold the sit for even your most enthusiastic friend.

Teaching the Down

The down command means lay down and be still. It does not mean lay down and crawl or lay down and wrestle. It is vitally important that your dog know the down command and respond to it immediately. In an emergency, a quick response to a down could save you precious seconds. For example, in a nursing home, the person you are visiting might have a medical emergency or might start to fall. If your dog responds to your down command immediately, you could catch the falling person or call for help without worrying about what your dog is doing or whether he is in the way.

1. With your dog sitting at your left side, sit or kneel next to him and reach over his shoulders with your left arm. Take hold of his left front leg with your left hand and his right front leg with your right hand. As you command him, "Jake, Down,"

The down command, when used with the stay, teaches the dog to control himself and be still in distracting circumstances. (Although, the Doberman seems to have taken this lesson a bit too far!)

lift both front legs slightly and pull them forward, gently laying him down on the ground. Transfer your left hand to his shoulder so that if he tries to get up, you can stop him with a bit of gentle pressure. Interrupt any crawling or sniffing with a verbal "Acck!" Follow with praise. When you're ready for the dog to get up, pat him lightly on the rib cage and tell him "OK!" and "Sit!"

2. With your dog in a sit by your left side, reach over with your left hand and arm as in Step 1 and pull the left leg out as you give him the down command. *Use your right hand to signal the down command by moving your hand from the dog's nose to the ground.* Put your left hand on his shoulder to prevent movement, as in Step 1. Praise him when he's down.

3. With your dog in a sit, give him the down command and, at the same time, the down signal with your right hand. *Instead of reaching over him with your left hand, put your left hand on his shoulder. Don't push down, simply rest it there.* Praise him for laying down.

4. With your dog in a sit, give the down command and signal, keeping your left hand off the dog entirely. Praise him for laying down.

5. With your dog in a down, have someone walk up to him and reach as if to pet him. Correct him if he tries to get up or if he crawls toward the person. Continue practicing until your dog will remain down while someone walks up to pet him.

Teaching the Stay

The stay command means that you want your dog to hold his position and not move until you tell him it's okay to move. This exercise can be difficult for many dogs to learn, but this a very important command. When the dog is solidly trained to do a sit-stay or down-stay, you can open a door and know that your dog isn't going to dash through it. You can help someone into their bed or wheelchair and know that your dog will not impede your efforts. There are dozens of practical uses for the stay and it is the foundation exercise for many advanced obedience commands.

1. Ask your dog to sit by your left side. Hold the leash in your left hand, close to his collar. Don't hold the leash tight. Give the stay signal—right hand open, palm toward your dog's face, move your hand up and down about three inches in front of his nose, as if you were building an invisible wall, and give the command, "Stay." Pivot and take one step so

The dog needs to understand that the stay means to hold still. Start by teaching the stay when you are close to the dog and he is on a leash. Later, you can increase the distance between you and your dog.

that you are standing in front of him. Count to three, then step back beside him, praise and then release him.

If your dog moves from the sit prior to you releasing him, give him a quick "Acck!" and reposition him. If he jumps up from the sit while you are praising him, but before you have released him, again, give him a verbal interruption ("Acck!") and reposition him in the sit.

In this first step, make sure that you make him hold the stay for no longer than a count of three seconds. If you ask him to hold the stay too long and too soon, he will not learn the exercise as quickly.

2. With your dog sitting at your left side, command him to stay as you give him the stay signal, and then pivot and move one step in front of him. Wait *ten seconds* then return to his side, praise him, and release him.

3. Continue the sit-stay for ten seconds, *but move three steps in front of your dog.* Praise him and release him.

4. Move three steps away, but increase the time of the stay to *fifteen seconds*. Praise him and release him.

5. Very gradually, over several training sessions, increase the time you ask your dog to hold the stay to *one minute*. Praise him and release him.

6. Very gradually, over several training sessions, increase the distance you move from your dog to *ten steps away.*

If your dog is having trouble, go back a step or two, review the first steps again, and very gradually work your way back up to a longer stay.

Teach the down-stay in the same manner. Alternate training sessions with the sit-stay and the down-stay and make sure you go through all of the training steps with both of the exercises.

Keep in mind that stays are very difficult for a dog to learn and require a great deal of self-control on his part. Do two or three training steps, with an enthusiastic release after each one, and then go on to something else. Let your dog succeed.

Teaching the Walk on a Leash

Your dog needs to understand that the leash is not something with which to fight or play. There are several ways to reinforce this. Practice all of them.

Leash Awareness

1. With your dog on leash, back away from him the entire six-foot length of leash. If he looks at you, praise him. If he follows you, praise him even more. If he looks away from you, back up quickly and lightly snap the leash (just enough to get his attention) and comment to him in a high-pitched, surprised tone, "Wow! What happened?" Praise when he reacts to the snap and your voice by looking at you or, even better, following you, as you continue to back away.

2. Continue backing up in an erratic, zigzag manner. If your dog starts watching you out of the corner of his eye as he continues to sniff or look around, *use a verbal correction* ("Acck!") as well as a snap of the leash. Make sure you praise him when he follows you.

3. If your dog catches on to this game and is trotting with you, face to face with you as you back away, *stop and have him sit in front of you,* and praise

him enthusiastically! That is exactly what you want him to do!

Watch Me

The watch-me command teaches your dog to pay attention to you. This premise might seem overly simple, but if your dog doesn't pay attention to you, his lack of attention could cause him to miss other commands or directions you might give him.

1. With your dog sitting in front, facing you, hold the leash in one hand and gather up the slack. Hold a treat in the your other hand. Let him see the treat and sniff it. Take the treat from his nose and bring it to your face as you tell him "Jake, Watch Me!" As soon as his eyes flick to you, praise him ("Yeah! Thank you! Good boy!") and then pop the treat in his mouth.

Wilma does a nice watch-me, making eye contact with Jane.

Always give the verbal praise *first,* for two reasons. First, your dog will eventually work by voice command alone. Second, your timing is much better by using verbal expression than by physical expression.

2. With your dog sitting in front of you, tell him "Watch Me" and *begin backing away from him.* Encourage him to follow you and praise him when he does. Move the treat back and forth between you and the dog a couple of times if he gets distracted. Take only a few steps backwards, then stop. Ask him to sit, repeat the command, and reward him when he responds.

3. Repeat as in Step 2, except *increase the distance that you back up.* Back in a zigzag pattern, challenging your dog to follow you. Use your voice to encourage him to follow. Then stop, have him sit in front of you, and reward him.

4. *Have your dog sit by your left side, his right shoulder by your left leg.* Bend around slightly so that he can see your face and give him the watch-me command.

Beginning the Heel

The heel command means that your dog should walk by your left side, with his right shoulder aligned with your left leg. He is to maintain this position as you walk together.

1. Make sure that your dog thoroughly understands Steps 3 and 4 of the watch-me exercise. Repeat Step 3 of the watch-me and then, as you are backing up from him, *turn while you are walking so that you end up facing straight ahead and your dog moves up to your left side.* As he moves into position, tell him "Jake, Heel! Watch Me! Good

Wilma, a Weimaraner, demonstrates a good heel position.
She is walking nicely by Jane's side, without pulling.

boy!" Use your voice and his motivator (if necessary) to encourage him to keep this position and to continue watching you. After you have walked six to ten feet, stop, have him sit, and praise him.

2. Repeat as in Step 1 except *walk fifteen to twenty feet* before you stop your dog and have him sit.

3. Repeat Step 2 and *add left and right turns* to your walking pattern. This is one of the most important steps for teaching a good, enthusiastic heel. Don't rush this one. If your dog doesn't understand or is fighting the leash or you, don't get impatient. Simply go back to Step 1 and start again.

Teaching the Come

The come command means that your dog should drop everything he's doing and come directly to you as fast as he can. To teach your dog to come quickly every time you call, there are a couple of rules that everyone in the household needs to follow. First of all, never command him to come and then punish him. If, for instance, he chews up the chaise lounge cover when you leave him in the backyard, don't call him to you to punish him. He's not going to associate the punishment with the act of chewing up the chaise lounge cover. He will associate the punishment with the last thing that happened—you calling him to come. Second, never call him to come and then do something nasty to him like give him a flea bath. He will see it as punishment.

1. With your dog on the leash, simply back away from him and command him, "Jake, Come!" Back up about ten feet, as quickly as you can without tripping, and praise your dog when he follows you. Give him a treat.

2. Repeat Step 1, but stop and have your dog sit in front of you. Praise and reward him when he does.

If at any time your dog does not follow you, snap the leash to get his attention, continue to back away from him, and encourage him to follow you.

6

What Special Training Is Needed?

Therapy dogs may have to do a variety of tasks for which additional training is needed, if for no other reason than to make sure accidents don't happen. Enhanced or special training should be taught by following the step-by-step method detailed in Chapter 5. Remember, introduce each command in small training steps, setting your dog up for success rather than failure. For example, when teaching your dog to walk up steps, have him step up one stair first, coaxing him with a treat if necessary, then praise and reward him. If learning the stairs seems to be a problem, praise him for ascending each step for six or seven steps. When he's got the hang of it and is more confident, go three or four steps before rewarding him. Keep training sessions upbeat, encouraging, and very positive.

Socialization

Therapy dogs must be people dogs. This is achieved by exposing the dogs to people of every age, size, shape, and ethnic background. Don't assume that because you are taking your dog to a nursing home that he only needs to be exposed to the elderly. Children and adults visit nursing homes.

Regular visits to a variety of places, including parks and shopping centers, allow dogs to meet a variety of people.

*The Love on a Leash therapy dog group takes their dogs
to the streets to train. The dogs meet all types of people, learn to
behave in public, and learn to be good around each other.*

Encourage people to pet your dog and explain his job. These visits accomplish two things: people learn more about therapy dogs and your dog benefits from a lot of socialization.

Therapy dogs recognize different types of people. Gracie is a Basset Hound that has been a therapy dog for several years. She visits nursing homes and convalescent centers, and usually meets with the elderly. During one socialization visit to the mall, Gracie's owner, Pam Posey, noticed a group of senior citizens coming into the mall, several of them in wheelchairs. Gracie saw them a moment later and alerted to them, straining at her leash, staring at them and whining. Pam commented, "Her whole attitude seemed to say, 'Those are the people I'm supposed to see! That's my job!'"

Exposure to Equipment

A moving wheelchair or walker can be a frightening thing to a dog that has never seen one. Introduce your dog to a walker or wheelchair so that he looks on it as a positive thing, rather than something about which to be nervous.

If you have a wheelchair or walker available for training, put a dog biscuit on it and let your dog walk up and take it. Encourage him, "Go ahead! Where's the cookie? Find it!" Do not drag the dog up to the walker by his collar. Let him walk up to it on his own. When he gets the cookie, praise him.

Repeat this exercise, but add motion. Move the walker or wheelchair (rattle it and roll it) a few feet, then hide a

Misty walks alongside Rich and the wheelchair so that she is familiar with the sight and sound of it moving.

cookie again and ask your dog to find it. When he's got the idea that the wheelchair or walker is the source of goodies, repeat the exercise, but this time drop the wheelchair to the ground on its side, hiding a cookie as you do so. Immediately, before your dog gets worried about the noise, coax him to the wheelchair, "Where's the cookie? Find it!"

When your dog is comfortable with the noise of the equipment, start walking with the chair or walker. Push it ahead of you and have your dog walk or heel with you. Encourage him to keep up with you, "Good boy to walk with me!"

When your dog is following the wheelchair with no problem, ask someone to sit in it. Have them hand the dog a cookie and say, "Good boy!" When your dog willingly

Rich gives Misty a treat, encouraging her to step in closer to the wheelchair.

approaches someone sitting in a wheelchair, teach him to come to the chair for petting and, at the same time, teach him to avoid the wheels and foot pegs. Do this by teaching him to approach the front of the big side wheel, but behind the front wheels and to the side and rear of the foot pegs. Teach him to approach from either the left or right, so that people with a nonfunctioning arm (or hand) can pet him with their other hand.

Also introduce your dog to canes and crutches. Let him see them in use, laying on the floor, and propped up against furniture. Drop them to the ground so that he can hear the noise they make when dropped. If he's bothered by the noise, do the hidden cookie routine.

Expose your dog to rolling carts and gurneys, respirator equipment, vacuum cleaners, and other equipment with which he is unfamiliar. Train him not to be startled by this equipment.

Exposure to Different Surfaces

Some special training is needed in an area about which one might not immediately think. A therapy dog will come into contact with a variety of surfaces (slippery floors, all types of furniture, and laps) and must be trained on how to interact with them without injuring himself or the person he is visiting.

Slippery Floors

Many dogs react to slippery floors by arching their feet and extending their nails. This posture gives them traction in snow and mud, but on a slippery floor, it makes things worse. A dog doesn't realize that his pads can give him better traction on a slippery floor than his nails.

Good foot grooming is essential to good traction. Keep the hair between his pads trimmed short and keep his nails reasonably short. Don't cut into the quick, of course, but keep his nails trimmed back so that when he stands normally, the nail is not touching the floor.

When teaching your dog to walk on slippery floors, have him stand still until he relaxes. Don't force him to move forward while his feet are arched and the nails are extended. He can't hold that foot position long, so let him stand until he relaxes. Then, encourage him to walk. Don't put any pressure on the leash at all; don't pull it or snap it. Let him work on his balance without your interference. When he's willing to walk on the slippery floor on his own, encourage him to walk faster or farther by using your voice, "Good boy! Come on!" or by holding a treat in front of his nose. Praise him for being brave when he's walking well.

Chairs

Occasionally you can invite your dog up on furniture, but don't do this as a general rule. The housekeeping staff will not be happy about the extra cleaning to get the dog hair off the upholstered furniture. If there is a straight-backed wooden chair or vinyl chair, you might invite your dog to sit on that. Teach him that an invitation to get up on a chair means to get up in the chair carefully, turn, and sit still.

Beds

You need to teach your dog to get up on and down from a bed gracefully, so that when commanded to do so, he can do it without hurting himself or the person being visited. A bedridden patient may not be able to reach your dog and may ask for him to get on the bed. Make sure you get permission from the activities director or other staff members *prior* to allowing the dog up on the bed. Many facilities have very strict ideas about where the dogs should be allowed and beds are often off-limits to dogs.

Rules need to be established and maintained. Is the dog allowed up on a bed or not? Don't let residents sabotage training efforts.

Teach this command at home first, then practice it at a friend's house (a different bed) before attempting it during a visit. Teach your dog that "Up!" means jump carefully, where directed by your hand, and then hold still. "Crawl" is a useful command to guide the dog within reach of a hand. Use an extra sheet or a big towel to protect the bedding and have him lay on the towel. Small dogs can be lifted onto the bed where they can be petted. Again, they need to be taught to stay still.

Laps

Small dogs can be lifted into laps, but only after asking the person if the dog is wanted on the lap. Some people like to pet and hug dogs, but don't want them on them. Other people will ask for a big dog to come in their lap. Beware of this request. Obviously, the physical well-being of the person comes first. A large dog could break fragile bones, never mind bruise or scratch the person being visited.

When in a lap, your dog should sit still until he is lifted down. Never allow him to jump down on his own, as a slippery floor could cause him to hurt himself.

Special Commands

There are a variety of special commands to teach your therapy dog. A few of them are listed in the following

Zippy is a little heavy to sit in laps, so she has learned to put her feet up in a lap. Here she watches Charlie open a birthday present.

pages. But, be original! If you recognize the need for appropriately trained behavior in a specific situation, make up a short command and use it to teach your dog how to act accordingly.

"Watch Your Step!"

Teach your dog a command that means watch your step. During your training sessions, away from the hospital or nursing home, place a ladder flat on the ground and encourage your dog to walk the length of the ladder. Make sure he steps over the rungs. Tell him, "Watch Your Step!" If he stumbles or trips, correct him ("Acck! Watch Your Step!") and point to the rungs so that the dog is looking at them.

When he can walk the ladder without tripping, take a garden hose and drape it between two chairs about six inches off the ground. Point to it as you tell your dog "Watch Your Step!" and walk him over the hose. If he trips, lower the hose and try again.

During a visit, if there is something on the ground, tell your dog to watch his step and point to the object to be avoided or stepped over.

"Feet Up!"

"Feet Up!" is a good command with many uses for therapy dogs. If your dog can lift his front feet up to the rail of the wheelchair or to the side of the bed, people can reach to pet him more easily. Practice this command when there is no one in the chair, so that your dog won't scratch people or accidentally land in their lap. Tell him "Feet Up!" as you tap the arm of the chair. Help him lift his front feet up and place them on the arm of the chair. If he's unsteady, use your leg to brace his back legs. (Always brace his hind legs with your leg when he is on his hind feet on a slippery floor.)

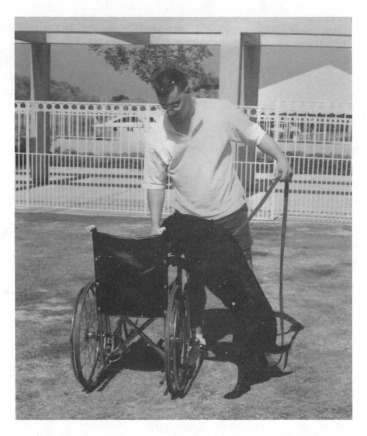

*Misty learns to put her feet up on the armrest of the
wheelchair so that the occupant may pet her easily.*

When your dog knows this command with a chair, try
the same command on the side of the bed, the arm of a
couch, and on bedside rails. Be ready to catch him if he
tries to jump up onto the bed and, whatever you do, don't
laugh if he does! If he thinks it's funny, he'll jump up again
and perhaps hurt someone.

When you have your dog execute this command when
visiting, always make sure the person being visited knows
what your dog is going to do so that she is not frightened.
It's also important that you move that person's hand or

Laurie has Sam put his feet up on her arm so that he doesn't scratch Margaret when he gives her a kiss on the cheek.

arm out of the way so that your dog's paws land on the chair arm instead of the person's arm.

"Be Still"

One of the most important commands that a therapy dog needs to know is the be-still command. Teach the dog that this means do not move at all. This command is more strict than the stay command. "Be Still!" means your dog should "freeze." You will use this command in a variety of situations, such as when a frightened child wants to touch the dog and movement might scare the child even more or when an elderly person with poor balance wants to walk past the dog. Teach this command to your dog just as you would the stay command, except keep your hands on your dog so that you can hold the body part that starts to move.

"Go!"

Your dog must also learn the go command. This command is invaluable during a medical crisis or when someone just doesn't feel up to his company. Teach your dog to walk out of the room quietly and sit by the door.

Other Commands

As you work with your dog, you might discover other commands that you want to teach him. Go ahead! If you wish him to hold still so that someone can brush him, teach him a command for it.

If you wish to teach him how to ride in an elevator without being nervous, walk him into the elevator, give him a treat, and walk him out. Next, walk him into the elevator, close the doors (but don't go anywhere), give him a treat, and open the doors and walk out. Then, when he is comfortable with this exercise, take a short ride (one floor). Create a training program based on small, progressive steps and your dog can learn just about anything.

Trick Training

Trick training is not required for therapy dogs, but it is a lot of fun. Mandy, a Cocker Spaniel mix, loves to perform her tricks and will even initiate them herself. She dances, sits up and waves, jumps through a hoop, and even does complicated routines. During therapy dog visits or socialization trips, the tricks are great ice breakers, giving people a chance to smile, laugh, and applaud. And Mandy, of course, loves the attention.

Lauren and Mandy practice their trick training. Tricks are fun to teach, fun for the dog to perform, and are very entertaining.

The therapy dog is effective because he is being shared and presented by a caring owner. The dog does not work alone—the person on the other end of the leash is half of the team.

What Do You, the Dog's Partner, Need to Know?

Your primary objective, as the therapy dog's owner and partner, is to share your dog with other people in a way that stimulates emotional well-being, promotes healing, and improves the quality of life for the people being visited and the staff that cares for these people. All in all, you try to share all the benefits of owning a dog.

To be an effective therapy dog partner, you must like people just as much as your dog likes them. If you are reserved, shy, angry, or defensive, the reactions from the people being visited may be inhibited. Be outgoing, friendly, and happy in a way that is natural to you. Don't be afraid to give someone a hug or to touch their hand. Be warm and caring, never condescending.

Show the people you visit that you care about them. Express your feelings by your body language, smile, and words. Caring is not something that can be faked; it comes from the heart.

Know Your Dog

It's vitally important that you know your dog and can anticipate his reactions in certain situations. For example, Eva Shaw knows that her Welsh Terrier, Zippy, is leery of children in certain situations. Zippy is over her fear of kids, but Eva knows that if kids are running around and yelling, such as on a school playground, Zippy will become anxious.

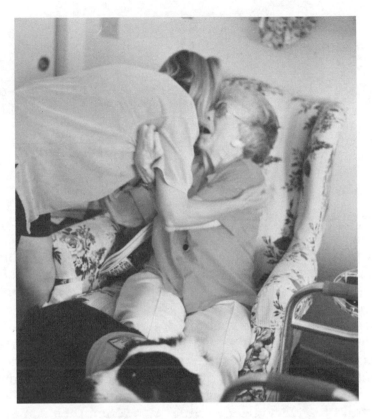

*A partner must show, in expression, manner, or action,
that she cares about the people she is visiting.*

By being aware of her dog's reactions, Eva can either avoid visits with many children or be prepared to handle any interactions between excited kids and Zippy so that nothing negative happens. By knowing your dog and being aware of how he reacts in certain situations, you can prevent any problems or accidents.

Know the People You Are Visiting

It's important that you know something about the people and facility you are visiting. If you are visiting an Alzheimer's

A partner must ensure that her dog is well trained and ready to visit. Joan is reviewing some of DC's basic commands, including lay down.

care facility, it's important to have some knowledge of the disease so that you can react appropriately. The same goes for a mental health facility, a children's special education classroom, and so forth. Don't be afraid to ask questions of the staff. Ask them what you can expect to see when you visit the facility. Ask them about potential problems, reactions, or behaviors. In most cases, the staff will be more than happy to help you and might even recommend some reading material that can help you understand the people with whom you will visit.

Patients with Alzheimer's Disease

Alzheimer's disease is a progressive, degenerative disease of the brain and is eventually fatal. The cause is still unknown and research is ongoing. The disease is progressive, which means that it gets worse over a period of time. Some of the most common symptoms of the disease include depression, memory loss, changes in concentration,

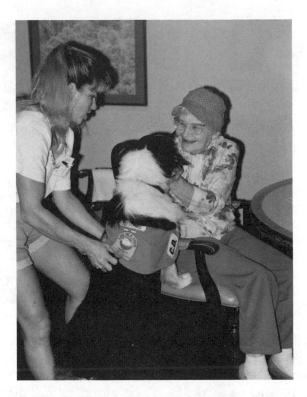

*A partner must present her dog to the person being visited so that
both the dog and ther person are comfortable with the situation.
(Michelle Lund and her Australian Shepherd, Hugs.)*

confusion, and moodiness. Many Alzheimer's patients are
prone to wandering and must be constantly supervised or
kept behind locked doors. Judgment is impaired and for-
getfulness is common.

Most Alzheimer's patients go through different stages of
the disease and exhibit different behavior during each
stage. Confusion, anger, frustration, and fear are very common behaviors, and you must be able to deal with these
severe emotional swings. Someone that has previously visited with the therapy dog may suddenly hate the dog. Don't
take offense, simply walk away and offer to visit again
another day.

A Cautionary Word

If someone does not want to visit with a therapy dog, that wish should be respected. Some people are allergic to dogs or are very afraid. Also, as much as it may be foreign to those of us who love dogs, there are people who simply do not like dogs. Although we may disagree with their view of dogs, their wishes should be respected.

Many Alzheimer's patients benefit tremendously from a visit from you and your therapy dog. Try and read the patient's mood. If a visit is welcomed, encourage the person to talk. Many times, long-term memory is still vivid and sharp, and talking about these memories makes the person feel wanted and important. Ask about the dogs this person has known. If those memories are lost, ask how your dog makes the person feel.

When initiating a conversation, ask simple questions that can be answered with a yes or no. Repeat pertinent pieces of your conversation; memory joggers are good. Keep the conversation pleasant, upbeat, and enthusiastic.

Be sensitive to the person being visited. Sometimes conversation is stressful. In these cases, simply allowing them to pet and hold the dog is the best medicine you can offer.

Stroke Victims

More than 25,000 people a year suffer from strokes. Strokes occur when the blood flow to a portion of the brain is disrupted, either by a clot or by a hemorrhage. Because every stroke is different as to severity and location within the brain, no two stroke survivors are the same and more than half of them are severely disabled.

Stroke victims often have speech impairments that may make it difficult for you to communicate. Apologize if you don't understand and try to read body language and hand movements to better understand what the person is trying to convey. Never pretend to understand when you really don't. The stroke victim could be trying to ask a question or convey important information. An inappropriate reply is unfair.

Most stroke patients enjoy therapy dog visits and the stimulation can help their physical therapy. Let them run a brush down your dog's back if they are able. This is a good exercise in dexiterity and strength. Ask the physical therapist if there is anything you and your dog can do to help.

The Developmentally Disabled

Developmentally disabled (or mentally challenged) individuals can vary in abilities, both mentally and physically. The severely retarded are limited in their ability to take care of themselves and to make decisions. Some may have physical disfigurements, some may be incontinent, and some may drool.

Never express negative emotion because of a person's appearance or their behavior. Be aware of your expressions; many times a subconscious thought is betrayed inadvertently.

Protect your dog should the person become too excited or get too rough. If the person has limited physical dexterity, place the dog's rump or side toward the person. This gives a larger surface to be petted and protects your dog's eyes and ears from poking fingers or rough handling.

The Visually Impaired

Always talk to a blind person as you approach so she knows where you are and she isn't startled. Talk in a normal tone of voice. For some reason, blindness is often associated with deafness and many people raise their voice when talking to a visually impaired person. Never assume that the person is also hearing impaired.

Always ask if the blind person needs help. Don't assume that she does. Many visually impaired people are very self-sufficient. If the blind person is to walk with you, offer *your arm* instead of taking hers.

When offering your dog to be petted, *ask* if you can have her hand to guide it to the dog. As she pets the dog, describe it to her. "Jake is an eight-year-old Australian Shepherd. He is primarily black with a white stripe up his nose, between his eyes." And so on. When you have finished your visit, talk to her as you leave. Let her know that you are leaving and tell her when you will return.

The Hearing Impaired

Hearing impairments vary from individual to individual and can range from a mild loss to total deafness. Always speak directly to hearing impaired people so that they can read your lips. Don't exaggerate your mouth as you talk. Instead, speak normally and face the person to whom you are talking. Never turn away in midsentence; this is considered very rude.

If the person isn't looking at you when you wish to start a conversation, lightly touch her on the hand or shoulder and make eye contact with her, then start speaking. Don't hesitate to write notes if you are having a communication problem.

Seniors

Some of the elderly you visit may have some health problems that require them to reside in a nursing home or convalescent center. Others may be hale and hearty and live in a retirement village to be close to people their own age. When you visit seniors, never assume that the person is ill or senile. Instead, approach each person as an individual. Ask the staff for help if you have any questions as to how to approach a particular individual.

Children

Never leave a child unattended with any animal. Children often have good intentions, but may hurt an animal by being too rough or because they have not been taught how to handle an animal properly. Children also react to their emotions more readily than adults, or act out their feelings. Sometimes they hurt people and animals without actually meaning to hurt them.

Introduce the child to your dog by telling her your dog's name, its breed, its age, and anything else that might initiate a conversation. "Hi, this is Jake. He's an eight-year-old Australian Shepherd. He likes to herd sheep. Do you know what sheep are?"

Show the child how to pet the dog and encourage touching. If the child seems to like interacting with your dog and is withdrawing from you, don't try to continue a conversation. Supervise her, but also let her interact with your dog as much as possible.

If the child acts inappropriately, discourage it by talking about the dog's reactions. "Jake is afraid when people hit him." Substitute other actions. "Why don't you throw the tennis ball for Jake? He likes to chase it."

Young children often worry about what will happen when the dog leaves the facility, where it will sleep, who will feed it, and who will play with it. Answer all questions realistically and positively. Show the child that you take care of your dog and he is well loved.

Severely traumatized children often relate to a dog or other animal much better when an adult isn't actively involved in the conversation with them. Social workers, counselors, psychologists, and crisis intervention workers have used dogs with great success, by allowing a child to pet and talk to the dog without interference over a number of visits. After the child has a rapport with the animal, the professional can interject a question, perhaps phrased to include the dog, that will help them to better understand the child and facilitate her healing process. Sometimes a counselor will simply record the conversations that the child has with the dog. In either instance, your job is to stay unobtrusively in the background and ensure your dog behaves. Use gentle admonishments (a quiet "No!") to correct inappropriate behavior by your dog. You don't want to upset the child or "break the spell" of the visit.

Wheelchair Etiquette

When talking to someone in a wheelchair, sit down or kneel so that you are talking to the person face to face

Children need space to relate to your dog on their own terms. Photo by Click the Photo Connection.

instead of looking down at her. When someone has been using a wheelchair for a period of time, that chair becomes part of their personal space. Don't lean on the chair, sit on the arm of it, or move it without asking them first. *Never* pat the person in the chair on the head. Treat the person in the chair as you would like to be treated if you were using one.

Starting a Conversation

Although the primary objective of your visit is to share your dog, you are also a vital part of the interaction. Many times, you will need to initiate a conversation and draw the person out so that she can enjoy your dog.

Social workers and counselors use a technique called *active listening.* This technique uses the emotions of the person being visited as a basis for conversation and eliminates any judgments or opinions from you, the counselor, or other professional. This technique encourages participation in conversation and, when used properly, does not inject dead ends into the conversation. For example, if the nursing home resident says, "I used to have a dog. My daughter has my dog now." You can say, "Do you miss your dog?" The resident might reply, "Yes, I do miss him. He kept me company when my husband passed away."

Key phrases to use when conversing are: you think, you wish, you feel, you mean, and you like. These phrases assure the person that you really are listening and that you care. You react to what they say. You neither judge nor give unsolicited advice.

Coping with Grief

As you visit people in nursing homes or other care facilities and establish a regular routine, you will get to really know the people you visit and, perhaps, will make strong friendships with some of the residents. It's good for you and for the residents that you *do* care. Your caring shows that you are making a connection with them. Unfortunately, caring also leaves you open to grief when these people pass away. Grieving allows you to come to terms with the death of someone about whom you care. It helps you to heal. Don't be afraid to show your grief to family members of the deceased. It may help them to know that you care enough to grieve.

Unfortunately, your therapy dog will grow old, too, and pass away. Our dogs' lives are much too short. The sorrow that a dog owner suffers when a treasured pet dies or is euthanized is just as painful as when a family member dies, and the grief that follows is just as strong. Grief can cause physical changes, including insomnia and eating disorders.

In memory of Chocho.
When an old therapy dog dies, the grief is just as strong as when a family member dies.

Many times you will start to grieve even before the person or dog passes away. When your treasured therapy dog is growing old or when a favorite resident's health is failing, you know what is going to happen. This initial grieving is called *anticipatory grief*. It might not be today or tomorrow, but death is inevitable.

Other stages of grief include denial: "No, Melba hasn't passed away; she's in the hospital." There are different types of denial, ranging from nonacceptance of the death to modified denial, including being dishonest with yourself. Anger, bargaining, and depression are three other stages of grief. People question their faith, try to make bargains with God, or they scream at the attending physician. As long as you don't let your anger get out of control, releasing it can relieve stress and tension. However, don't let anger and depression consume you. Seek help in coping with your loss.

Help is available not just for family members, but also for friends of the deceased and professionals involved with death, including therapy dog partners. Hospice programs have grief support groups, as do many mental health programs.

While you are grieving, it's important that you be kind to yourself. Be gentle. Grieving takes time. There are no quick fixes. You cannot tell yourself: Okay, I've cried. It's over. Everyone has their own emotional timetable and some heal faster than others. Let yourself grieve and don't be afraid to ask for help.

Some therapy dog partners, after grieving for a resident that has passed away, will then shut themselves off from other residents so that they will not have to feel the pain of grieving again. This is a natural reaction, but it is not good for the other residents. They will feel your reserve and not only will they withdraw from you, but you won't get as much out of the visit either.

Dog owners do the same thing. They think: I won't get another dog, so I won't be hurt when it dies. This is true, but you'll never again know the joy, comfort, and friendship that a dog can bring.

If a member of the therapy dog group is grieving, don't offer platitudes. Everyone has different beliefs about death. Simply say, "I'm sorry." Offer a shoulder to cry on, a hankie to wipe the eyes, and send a card to let her know that you care.

Grieving is hard. Losing someone you care about can be devastating. When you love, you give each person or dog a chunk of your heart. When they pass away, they take that piece of your heart with them, leaving a hole in your heart and immense sadness. You will *never* forget them, but the pain will soften and you will, once again, open your heart to love.

*Ursa's obvious affection brings a smile to Andy's face.
She has been visiting him twice a month for close to six years
and they both look forward to their time together.*

8

How Do You Get Started?

Visiting as an Individual

Many people do therapy dog work alone—just them-selves and a dog or two. This is especially beneficial if you work unusual hours and need to schedule volunteer work at different times.

Who Do You Want to Visit?

If you decide to work alone, before you actually start visiting, you need to decide who you want to visit. Do you want to take your dog to visit young children at day-care centers? Would you like to visit older children in schools and talk about responsible dog ownership and training? Would you like to visit special education classrooms and work with disabled kids? Would you like to visit hospitals or would you rather work with the elderly at nursing homes or retirement centers? When deciding *who* you would like to visit, take into consideration the people that your dog prefers. If he loves kids and does not get too excited by them, you might want to visit children.

How Much Time Can You Devote?

Once you have decided who you would like to visit, determine how much time you can spend on this project.

Remember to include not only visiting times in your figuring, but also take into account how long it takes you to groom your dog, travel to and from the facilities you might visit, and time to debrief or relax with teachers or staff after each visit.

How Often Can You Visit?

Your time estimate will impact the number of visits you make. Even if you have a lot of time, most people find that one to two one-hour or two-hour visits per week are about all they can handle emotionally. An emotionally satisfying visit can still be physically exhausting for both you and your dog.

Organize Your Data

Once you have figured out who you would like to visit and how often you can do it, you need to organize a presentation so that you can approach different facilities and discuss your ideas with the activities director. The presentation can be a letter explaining that you would like to visit the facility, what you plan to do during visits, and how often you can come. Include some background information about your preparation for these visits as well as information about your dog's training and unique talents.

Visiting as a Group

The most popular form of therapy dog work is a group. The group may be comprised of several people from the local dog-training club, volunteers from the local humane society, or it may simply be a group of people sharing the same interest.

To attract people for a new therapy dog group, talk to people. Tell the members of your dog-training club, tennis club, or even your bridge group what you would like to do.

Give a brief talk to social organizations such as the Kiwanis or Elks lodge to garner interest and group members. Talk to the staff at local nursing homes. You may find that staff members are dog owners and may be very interested in participating.

When you have a number of potential members, set a date for your first group meeting. At the meeting, explain what a therapy dog is and who benefits from therapy dogs. Indicate and demonstrate the training required of a therapy dog and explain the certification process. Don't forget to detail the therapy dog's partner's responsibilities, too.

At this point in the meeting, if people are still interested in being a part of a therapy dog group, ask for volunteers to help organize the group. Assign someone with dog-training experience to oversee the dogs' training and certification. Select a social director to approach activity directors, arrange visits, and schedule dogs for those visits. Ask someone to be in charge of fund raising so that you can print business cards, and make matching bandannas or vests for the dogs and their partners.

If the group is successful, you may decide to become more formal by electing officers and establishing a board of directors. If the group is successful in fund-raising, you may want to offer a small scholarship to a future veterinarian or health-care professional.

Approaching the Activities Director

Never drop in unannounced to present your group to the activities director. Call ahead and schedule an appointment. Be on time for your appointment and dress in a manner appropriate to a professional meeting. A nice pair of slacks and a shirt, and comfortable shoes are just fine.

Bring your dog with you so that he can help you sell the idea of a therapy dog group. Ask the activities director for permission to demonstrate some of your dog's skills by taking him out to meet some of the residents.

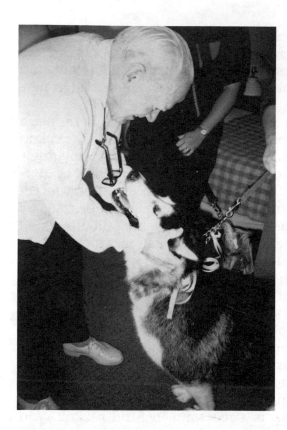

Bring your dog with you when you go to meet the activities director. A well-behaved dog is a great sales tool.

Bring copies of all of your relevant paperwork (such as therapy dog certifications and proof of insurance) so that the activities director has this information readily available when seeking management approval. Also bring a copy of your dog's vaccinations (including rabies) and any tests your veterinarian might have performed in preparation for your first meeting.

Reference materials are also good to bring along, especially if the activities director is unfamiliar with therapy dog work. Bring her a copy of this book or some additional reading material.

Don't expect the activities director to give you an immediate decision. Although she, personally, may be tremendously excited about having you visit her facility, she most likely needs to acquire management approval. Offer to obtain any other material she may need to present your proposal successfully to management.

When You Begin

When you have received permission to start your therapy dog program, go for a very short first visit to introduce your dog to the facility and to introduce the staff to your dog. During this preliminary visit, determine how and where you will meet with the people at this particular facility.

Introduce Your Dog to the Staff

The cooperation of the staff is of utmost importance to the success of your venture. Therefore, during your first visit, introduce yourself and your dog to the staff. Tell them why you are there and what you would like to accomplish. Ask for their feedback and any pointers they might have regarding specific residents. Tell them, realistically, what your dog can do. Offer to help whenever they feel that your dog might be of benefit in a particular situation.

When they know your schedule ahead of time, they can prepare a visit list of people who might be slightly depressed that day or who may need some extra motivation. Perhaps the counselor needs to talk to someone who is refusing to converse or the physical therapist is having trouble motivating someone to work a little harder. Your dog may help these professionals communicate.

Be prepared to answer the same questions over and over again (without getting impatient), as many of the staff will have the same questions, ideas, or fears: A therapy dog is . . . No, he won't bite. He loves people. Yes, please pet him; that's his job! No, he's not afraid of wheelchairs. He's been trained around them. If a staff member is afraid of your dog, don't force her to pet him or embarrass her because of her fears. You are more apt to win her over by allowing her to watch and see that your dog is gentle and that the residents enjoy him. She may approach you one day and ask to touch your dog.

Learn Your Way Around the Facility

When you first visit the facility, find the important areas. Locate the public restroom, the nursing station, the fire exits, the stairs and/or elevators, and all egresses to the building.

As you walk around, memorize the layout of the facility. You don't want to get lost. Are the hallways laid out in an H pattern? Is the nursing station the hub of a cluster of hallways? Is the A wing painted green and the B wing painted pink? If you think you might get lost, ask the activities director how she found her way around.

While you learn your way around the facility, let your dog look around, too. Let him get accustomed to the smells and sounds of the facility. Seek out potential trouble spots such as the noise of the garbage disposal in the kitchen and the microwave in the nurses' lounge.

Set Up a Schedule

When you have met the staff and familiarized yourself with the facility, talk to the activities director about setting up a schedule. Visiting the same facility two or three times a month works very well, although visiting every week is even better. Visiting this often allows you to get to know the residents, their moods, their likes and dislikes, including which dog they like best. You can also establish a better working relationship with the staff when you visit on a regular basis.

If the activities director would like you to come more frequently than you had planned, be realistic with her. Tell

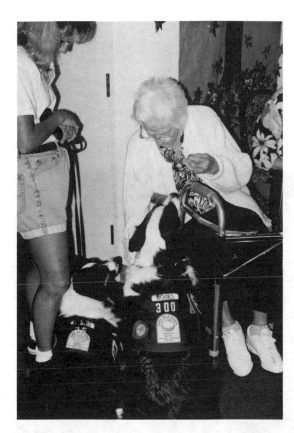

Hugs and Ursa vie for attention from a resident more than willing to give it to them.

her how long it takes you to prepare for a visit and don't let anyone pressure you into coming more often than you had planned. After you've been visiting a while, you may find that you have more time and can visit more often. If so, great, but start conservatively.

When setting up the schedule, don't plan on coming at the same time something else is scheduled. If a volunteer is leading a sing-along while you are trying to visit with your dog, everyone will lose—you, your dog, the volunteer, and the residents.

During a visit, residents get a chance to reminisce.
Photo by Judith Strom.

9

What Is a Visit Like?

What Happens During a Visit?

The primary objective of a therapy dog visit is to make it possible for the dogs to visit with the people who need them. The visit should be upbeat, happy, and enthusiastic but controlled.

A member of the Pets Are Wonderful therapy dog group describes their visits as a party. They go into each facility smiling, laughing, and obviously happy to be doing what they're doing. Before they leave, residents and staff are smiling, too.

How Many Dogs?

The Pet Parade Therapy Dog Group visits as a group. A visit might include six to sixteen dogs. Many other groups also attend en masse and find that it works very well for them. The number of dogs participating in a visit should be determined in conjunction with the activities director.

One of the benefits of visiting as a group is the variety of breeds, colors, and sizes—there is a dog to match everyone's tastes. Some people like big dogs; some prefer small ones. Some like hairy dogs; others like dogs with smooth coats.

When a group of dogs is available, a dog can spend more time with one person without feeling pressured to move along and visit everyone else. If a resident is having a tough day, your dog might be able to spend just a little extra time with her to help or inspire her.

A group also provides moral support for the dogs' partners. Visits can be emotionally draining and one person, like one dog, might easily feel overwhelmed. However, one dog alone can be of tremendous help to a staff member working with a resident who has a particular problem. A physical therapist, counselor, or psychologist may ask that your dog help in a one-on-one (dog–resident) situation.

How Many Residents?

The number of residents who participate in a visit also varies. Work out the details of "how many and who" with the activities director prior to each visit. A group of residents

Care Bear wears a clown costume . . .

. . . and Gracie vamps it up for Halloween. Costumes, bandannas, and bows make people smile.

relaxing in the recreation room can be visited by a group of dogs and have a great time. Often, a party atmosphere pervades. On special days and holidays, therapy dogs visit in costume. However, someone who is depressed or doesn't feel good might enjoy (or benefit from) the visit better if one dog joins her in the privacy of her room.

Many therapy dog groups start in the lobby or recreation room, visit with a group of residents, and then spread out to visit other residents in their rooms.

Visiting an Individual

A therapy dog can't do his best work until he approaches the person being visited. Sure, some people have a lot of fun watching dogs play and seeing them interact

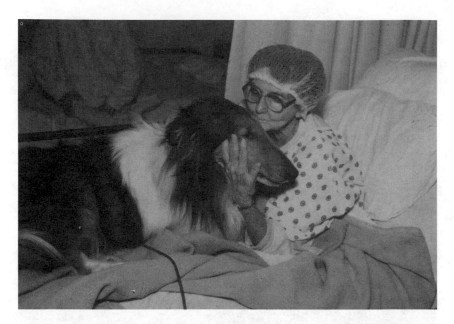

A gentle touch brings much-needed healing. Photo by Judith Strom

with other people, but one of the dog's best qualities is his ability to love and he needs to get close to people to do this.

When approaching someone, ask if they would like to see or pet your dog. Begin by asking, "Do you like dogs? Would you like to pet him?" If the resident says yes, introduce your dog: "This is Jake. He's an Australian Shepherd." Then let the conversation proceed naturally.

If the resident says yes, she likes dogs, but no, she doesn't want to touch him, you can still visit. Position your dog so that he is not touching the resident, but is within reach should she change her mind. Then initiate a conversation, starting by introducing your dog.

If the resident says that she doesn't like dogs, respect her opinion and move on to the next resident. However, recognize that some diseases affect verbal and communication skills and some residents may say no when they really mean yes. If a resident says no, watch carefully as you walk away. If the resident becomes upset or agitated, ask again, rephrasing the question. Ask the resident to move her hand or to nod her head if she wants to pet your dog.

Have your dog sit next to the wheelchair or chair, or put his feet up on the armrest. Remember to let the person know what your dog is about to do. If the person is in bed, have your dog put his feet up on the bedrails or, with permission of the staff and the resident, actually get up on the bed. If the resident is standing and looks somewhat weak or wobbly, ask the person to sit down so that your dog can visit, then help them to the nearest chair.

If the resident doesn't reach over to touch your dog, demonstrate by petting him yourself. Run your hand down your dog's head and neck as you explain: "He enjoys being petted. Would you like to pet him?" If the resident is not very responsive, gently take her hand and place it on your dog's head. If the resident resists, don't push! She may need to adjust to the visit before reaching out. Many times, the warmth and softness of the dog is enough stimulation to make the resident smile and begin petting your dog.

If someone, particularly a child, seems afraid of your dog, have your dog lay down and suggest that the person scratch your dog's tummy. Make your dog accessible to the resident. If there's a mobility problem, turn your dog around so that the person can pet his back. Sometimes petting the end without the teeth is less intimidating!

During a visit, you might want to allow the resident to give your dog a treat or, better yet, throw a ball or squeaky toy for him. Play is good for all of us, as is laughter, and watching a dog play makes a lot of people laugh.

Watching a dog do tricks is fun, too, and causes many people to laugh and clap. If your dog knows how to spin in a circle, jump through your arms, take a bow, or play dead, perform these tricks during your visit. People will respond.

If, during a visit, a resident wishes to hold or hug your dog, let them. Be quiet. Supervise the visit, but be unobtrusive. Allow the resident to pet, hug, and talk to the dog as much as he needs. If he wants to draw you back into the conversation, he will, but in the meantime, let your dog work his magic. Don't be afraid if the resident cries while hugging your dog. He may miss a dog that passed away or that he had to give away to come into the nursing home. Tears can be therapeutic.

Visiting a Group

If you have a group of residents that can gather in one place like the lobby, recreation room, or gym, put on a show for them. The show could be as simple as one dog doing an obedience demonstration or it could involve several dogs demonstrating a variety of dog sports, such as agility, flyball, and trick training.

A show gives the residents and the staff a chance to relax, laugh, and applaud. It breaks up their routine (in a positive way) and gives you a chance to show off your therapy dog!

Accounts of Actual Visits

The southern California chapter of the Love on a Leash Therapy Dog Program, Inc., schedules group visits one month in advance. To show you what visits can be like, let's follow several members of this group as they go about their volunteer work.

Alzheimer's Residential Care Facility

Ten dogs were scheduled to visit the local Alzheimer's residential care facility one Thursday morning. The dogs and their partners waited outside the facility until everyone was present. The dogs had been bathed, brushed, checked for fleas, been given a drink of water, and had a last chance to relieve themselves. When everyone was ready, they went inside.

Pam was in charge of the group and greeted the receptionist as she signed the group in, "Good morning! Are you ready for us?"

The receptionist, who had been waiting for the group, answered, "Of course we are! I'll let you in A wing first. Have a good visit."

After the receptionist unlocked the door to the A wing, the group filed in, careful to make sure none of the residents left while the door was open. (Many Alzheimer's patients are prone to wandering and the door is locked for their safety.)

The residents and staff awaited their visitors in the recreation room. As the dogs and their partners walked in, the partners greeted the group enthusiastically and then moved around the room, spreading out so that each resident could visit with a dog. (The group has been visiting this particular facility twice a month for almost eight years and have come to know many of the residents quite well.) Some of the staff approached the partners and requested that certain people be visited in their rooms, as they needed special attention that day.

Pam approached an elderly gentleman dressed in bright red sweatpants and sweatshirt.

"Good morning, Mr. Arthur. How are you this morning?" Mr. Arthur looked up at Pam but didn't answer.

Pam continued, "I brought Gracie to see you. Would you like to pet her?" Gracie, a Basset Hound, sat next to Mr. Arthur's chair, close enough so that he could reach her if he dropped his hand from the arm of the chair. When Mr. Arthur didn't reach toward Gracie as he normally did, Pam petted Gracie herself, saying, "Gracie just had a bath this morning and is very clean and soft. Feel how soft she is." With that suggestion, Mr. Arthur reached down to pet the dog. He started by petting the top of her head and then ran his fingers over her face, tracing the outlines of her black, tan, and white markings. He carefully stroked and handled each of her velvet-soft ears. All the while, Gracie sat as still as a statue, as if moving would cause Mr. Arthur to stop.

While Mr. Arthur petted Gracie, Pam was quiet, just watching. If he asked her a question, she would answer, but since she visited Mr. Arthur many times before, she knew that he didn't talk much and seemed to get more pleasure from touching the dog than from conversation.

Meanwhile, Sue's Irish Setter, Tara, was visiting with Thelma. Thelma loved to talk and was very animated, waving her arms and gesturing with her hands. Unfortunately, her case of Alzheimer's disease had progressed to the point that most of Thelma's conversations were gibberish, but she didn't realize it. As long as Sue smiled and responded with a comment once in a while, Thelma was happy. In between gestures and exclamations, Thelma reached down and hugged Tara enthusiastically. Whereas Mr. Arthur took pleasure in Gracie's company, Thelma needed both Sue and Tara.

The other dogs in the group were spread out, visiting individuals or small groups of people. Some of the volunteers had forged bonds with certain residents and always made sure to spend time with those people.

Beth and her Australian Shepherd, Max, have been visiting with the group for five years.

"My grandparents have all passed away," she said, "And I miss them. By visiting here and getting to know some of these people, I feel that I am giving back some of the love they gave me while they were alive."

After a half an hour, the group said good-bye to the residents, each in their own way. Sue knows that another person's touch is very important to Thelma, so she gave the older woman a hug as she told her, "I'll be back in two weeks. See you then." Pam didn't hug Mr. Arthur; however she did make eye contact with him and touched his hand as she said good-bye. The group moved on to another wing of the facility, where they followed the same routine. After an hour and a half (a half an hour per wing), the dogs and their partners were tired and ready to leave.

Alzheimer's Family Support Group

A couple times a year, the therapy dog group meets with the Alzheimer's family support group. During these gatherings, the therapy dog group introduces their dogs, explains what they do, and then answers questions. Many of the family members want to know how their loved one reacts to the dogs. Did Dad pay attention to the dog? Did Grandma pet the poodle?

This meeting gives the dogs' partners a chance to learn more about the people they visit. For example, Pam talked to Mr. Arthur's son and daughter-in-law and found out that Mr. Arthur used to have two Basset Hounds. That's why he enjoys Gracie's visits so much and reacts to her more than he does to the other dogs in the group.

Crisis Intervention

One day, Laurie Blaisdell, a member of the therapy dog group, called several members requesting help. She taught at the local middle school that her son attended. Recently, a young girl attending the school had been hit by a car and was killed at the school bus stop. A crisis intervention team and counselors were at the school talking with the children ,but several of the students were having a great deal of trouble talking about the incident. Laurie talked to the crisis intervention team leader and asked if he would like the therapy dogs to come in. He said, "Yes, definitely."

Six members of the group arrived at the school within hours of the request and reported to the crisis intervention team leader. He said, "I have several students who are refusing to admit that anything that has happened, a couple who won't talk at all, and one who didn't like the girl who died and is feeling very guilty. If you can spend some time with those kids, we can then see what happens."

Each of the kids and dogs interacted in different ways. One young boy was very active; sitting still was hard for him, especially under stress. Laurie took him aside with her active Australian Shepherd and she let the boy throw the Frisbee for Sam until they were both tired. Care Bear, a very sensitive, gentle dog was paired with a young girl who wouldn't talk. His gentle love and companionship could help her feel safe and protected.

Joan and her Newfoundland, Kody, took one of the students outside where she could throw a ball for Kody. After playing for a few minutes, Joan sat down and asked her dog to lay down on the ground. She told the young girl, "You know, when I was your age, I found it was much easier to talk to my dog about things that were bothering me than it was to talk to my parents. If you want to talk to Kody, you can. He can keep a secret and I promise I won't listen." With that, she pulled a book out of her pocket and pretended to read. She was still paying very close attention to both the child and Kody, but she didn't want the girl to know that. After a few minutes of sitting still, the girl slid closer to Kody and began talking to him in a quiet whisper. Within minutes, she was hugging the big dog tightly around the neck as she started to cry. Kody, responding to his training and perhaps even sensing her need, held still as she hugged him and cried. When her tears slowed down, he reached around and licked her face.

As the young girl's crying slowed, Joan beckoned a member of the crisis intervention team, who had been waiting and watching from the doorway. With Kody remaining as comfort and support, the counselor then began to talk to the young girl. With help from a big, black dog, the healing process started.

A Preschool Visit

Once a month, the group visits a local preschool. All of the children are younger than kindergarten age. During the visits, the dogs put on shows, do tricks, and generally

Bellvue's Broadway Trouper, CD, HC, TDI, VC during a Pet Care Lesson at a kindergarten class. Owned by Jane and Rick Wall.
Photo by Rick Wall.

entertain the children for a little while. Then, the children are allowed to pet and play with the dogs.

On one particular visit, the group brought agility equipment with them. Michelle explained what they would be doing. "This is our playground for our dogs. It's just like your playground. Watch Sam as he goes over the slide." With that, Laurie had her dog Sam climb up the small plastic slide and go down the other side. Michelle encouraged the kids to cheer and clap for the dogs as she continued introducing the dogs and the other obstacles—the A-frame, the teeter-totter, and the tunnels.

When they were through with the exhibition, she told the children they could play with the dogs and explained the rules. "Pet the dogs nicely on the head. Don't poke at their eyes or pull ears. You can throw the ball for the dogs but don't chase them." Twenty rambunctious kids and six dogs played for a half hour, running, screaming, barking, and generally having a good time.

Michelle tries to teach the kids something during each visit: how to approach dogs that they don't know, how to ask for permission to pet a dog, and how to care for their dog at home, including training and grooming. All of her instructions are geared toward the very young child, of course.

"I have a young daughter," Michelle said, "and having grown up with dogs, she is quite knowledgeable, telling her friends what to do and what not to do. But I would like more kids to know more about dogs. After all, these kids are our future."

Residential Nursing Home

The group has been visiting a residential nursing home for several years. In this facility, the residents are almost always in their rooms and the receptionist has a list of people who wish to see the dogs.

Linda and her Border Collie, Clio, had been visiting her Aunt Melba in the nursing home for several years. On this particular occasion, when Linda signed the visitor's book at the reception desk, the receptionist told Linda that her aunt was not doing well and other family members were already with her. When she approached her aunt's room, she knocked quietly on the door. "I don't want to intrude," she said to her uncle and cousins, "but Clio and I are here, should Melba want to see us."

"Please come in," Linda's cousin said. "Mom is fading in and out. I don't know if she'll acknowledge Clio, but let's try."

Linda told Clio "Up!" and the dog jumped up on the bed next to Melba. She pushed her long black and white nose under the woman's hand and as the dog did so, Melba smiled. Family members sighed and smiled to themselves. As they talked quietly, Clio snuggled up closer to the dying woman. Three hours went by as Linda and the other family members took turns talking, hugging, or simply sitting quietly. At different times, Linda asked Clio to leave the bed, but the dog wouldn't move, so she respected her desires. Finally, just as the sun was going down, Melba's hand moved on Clio's head. She gasped for air once and passed away. Giving her hand a quick lick, only then did Clio get down from the bed.

*Ursa loves to wear her vest, which sports her Therapy Dog
International patch, her Love on a Leash patch, a
Herding Instinct-certified patch, a Companion Dog obedience
title patch, and patches denoting the number of hours
she has served as a therapy dog.*

10

How Do You and Your Dog Become Certified?

What Is Certification?

Certification for therapy dogs is an assurance to activity directors, teachers, recreation staff, and management personnel that a dog has been properly screened, trained, and tested for therapy dog work so that accidents and injuries are kept to a minimum. Thorough screening, training, and testing eliminates dogs that don't have the temperament for therapy dog work. Certification can also qualify a dog and owner for insurance that covers the dog's actions during a visit.

Which Agencies Certify Therapy Dogs?

There are many organizations worldwide that organize visits with pets and certify dogs (or other pets) as therapy dogs. Each of the organizations have slightly different programs with different evaluation procedures. Points of contact for these organizations are included in the Appendix.

The Delta Society's Pet Partners Program

The Delta Society has been advocating the human–animal–environmental bond since 1976. This organization funds studies of the human–animal bond: how pets lower blood pressure, how dogs can help autistic children, how pets can stimulate those who have lost the desire to live, and so on. Some of these studies have provided the information needed to change housing laws that relate to pets and to allow pets in hospitals, where they were previously forbidden.

These studies are published in the society's educational and scientific journal, *Anthrozoos.* The Delta Society has a library of scholarly articles, videotapes, and other materials on the human–animal bond, and is expanding its database 130

The Delta Society has a set of standards and training information for animal-assisted therapy dogs and animal-assisted activity dogs. A training and evaluation course is available to prospective therapy dogs and their partners. This course covers obedience commands, temperament qualifications, and special training required. The Society also has standards for other animals, including exotic pets and farm livestock.

Love on a Leash Therapy Dogs

The Love on a Leash Therapy Dog Program, Inc., is a division of The Foundation for Pet Provided Therapy. Love on a Leash has established guidelines for screening, selecting, and training potential therapy dogs, and has a thorough evaluation process for the certification of qualified dogs.

Eva Shaw, one of the founding members of the group and presently serving on the board of directors, said:

> We would like everyone involved in the health-care fields to know that a dog certified by our organization is a stable, well-trained dog that is thoroughly qualified to be doing its wonderful work. (personal communication, 1994)

The program also stresses continuing education. Some of the recent issues of the organization's newsletter, *The Leash,* include information about Alzheimer's disease,

Please insert in **Love on a Leash**

Correction

Pages 125 and 128

Therapy Dogs Incorporated

Based in Wyoming, Therapy Dogs Incorporated has members all over the United States and Canada, with a network of Tester/Observers qualified to evaluate potential member/dog teams. TD Inc uses their own test to assess the appropriateness of each team for membership, after which they are required to be observed a minimum of three (3) times while actually working in a facility.

Page 130

TDI and the Delta Society also require the CGC test, while TD Inc uses their own test.

wheelchair etiquette, and how to talk to preschool-aged children. Other articles included dog-training information specific to therapy dog work.

This group also emphasizes continuing education for recreation personnel, activities directors, and teachers, so that these professionals can learn how therapy dogs could benefit them and their clients or students.

This group has training and evaluation guidelines that list the obedience and special training required for certification. Potential therapy dogs and their partners must also complete ten hours of supervised visits prior to certification.

Therapy Dog International

Therapy Dog International (TDI) is the oldest therapy dog organization in the United States. The founder, Elaine Smith, started TDI with her German Shepherd Dog, Phila. Elaine and Phila began making visits to nursing homes and hospitals in their local area in New Jersey. After many enthusiastic visits, Elaine realized that there were probably many people like herself, volunteering their time on an informal basis. In May 1980, Elaine unveiled to the world an organization dedicated to therapy dogs, Therapy Dogs International.

The goal of TDI is to unite and increase the numbers of therapy dogs, give them the recognition they deserve, and advertise on a national scale, alerting hospitals and other institutions to the importance of therapy dogs.

Potential therapy dogs must pass the American Kennel Club's (AKC's) Canine Good Citizen (CGC) test (which consists of ten obedience exercises, including sit, down, stay, and come) and be evaluated by a TDI representative.

Therapy Dogs Incorporated

Based in Wyoming, Therapy Dogs Incorporated (TDInc) has members all over the country. With emphasis on

Other Animals Can Provide Therapy, Too!

More and more therapy providers are realizing that all different types of animals foster the pet–people bond and **not all of them have to be warm and fuzzy either.**

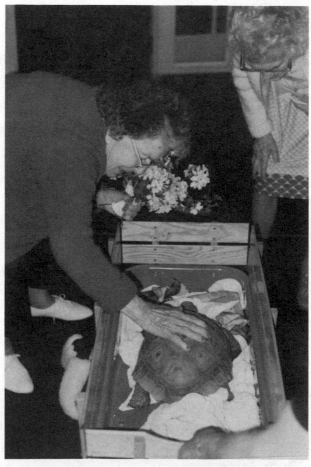

Tank, a sixty-year-old desert tortoise, creates quite a stir with the ladies!

A well-socialized ferret is an effective therapy provider.

Cats are also wonderful therapy animals. Flea made therapy visits for many years. His last visit was the week before he passed away, at the age of fourteen.

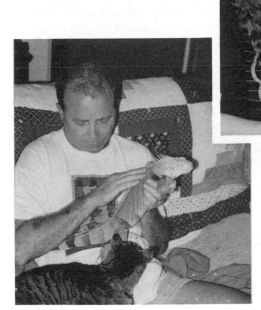

A cat and a . . . lizard?!? Sure! Comfort comes in all shapes and sizes.

thorough evaluation procedures for social therapy dogs, TDInc also requires that dogs pass the AKC's CGC test. In addition, each potential therapy dog must also pass the American Temperament Test Society's (ATTS) temperament evaluation. TDInc will supply a list of ATTS evaluators, or applicants can contact ATTS directly. During this evaluation, dogs are exposed to friendly strangers and aggressive strangers, as well as visual and auditory stimuli. The dog is encouraged to be curious, but should not show inappropriate aggression or fear. An evaluation form is then filled out and approved by a TDInc evaluator.

How to Certify You and Your Dog

The standards for certification differ in details from organization to organization. However, many of the standards are shared. The following lists some of the common factors shared by TDI and Love on a Leash, and other criteria suggested by other organizations that train or certify therapy dogs. Keep in mind, although most organizations have a minimum standard, your dog can never be *too* good, so don't train just for the minimum standards.

1. The dog must be screened for appropriate temperament and personality by an expert in dogs, dog behavior, or dog training.

2. The dog must be obedience trained and must react reliably to certain basic commands, including heel, sit, down, and stay.

3. The dog must undergo the specialized training needed to do the job. For example, the dog must know how to lift his feet up on the bedrails or the arm of a wheelchair so that people can reach to pet him.

4. The dog must be reliable around strange noises and sights, including any equipment with which

All certifying organizations reuire that a therapy dog be of the proper temperament: outgoing, friendly, and affectionate toward people.

he will come into contact at the facility where he is working.

5. The dog must be well socialized with people of all sizes, shapes, ages, and ethnic backgrounds.

6. The dog must be well mannered and reliable around other dogs and other pet animals.

7. The dog must be healthy and up to date on all vaccinations, including a current rabies vaccine.

8. The dog must be able to pass any specific health test required by the facility, included fecal exams, blood tests or skin cultures.

When you feel comfortable with your dog's obedience training and socialization, write to the therapy dog organization where you wish to certify your dog and ask for certification information. Also request information regarding an insurance policy for you and your dog.

TDI, TDInc, and The Delta Society all require that evaluations be performed by evaluators listed by their organization. A list of evaluators in your area will be sent to you along with the application for certification. Contact this person, who is usually a dog trainer, to schedule a meeting for the evaluation. All three agencies also require the CGC test. Many times, the evaluator can conduct the CGC test at the same time as the evaluation.

During the CGC test, the dog must demonstrate his ability to perform such basic obedience commands as the sit, down, stay, and come. The dog must also walk on the leash properly, without pulling or lunging, and ignore the approach of another dog. The dog must also accept the approach of a friendly stranger, the touch of a stranger, and combing (as if at a groomer's shop or a veterinarian's office).

Love on a Leash does not require the CGC test and allows applicants to use the dog trainer of their choice to conduct the obedience evaluation. Their evaluation is similar to the CGC test, but is directed more toward therapy dog work. The dog must demonstrate the basic obedience commands, but must also sit still for petting and hugging, and must be under control for visual and auditory stimuli (flapping plastic bag, a dropped metal pan).

Love on a Leash also requires ten hours of supervised visits to a nursing home or other facility. The applicant can contact a nearby facility, explain the process to the activities director, and set up a schedule to visit. After ten hours are completed, the activities director can then fill out the appropriate evaluation form.

Once all evaluations have been completed and signed, fill out the membership application, enclose any requested materials (e.g., TDI requires a copy of the CGC certificate, rabies certificate, and two photos of the dog), and return the materials, along with the required fee. In a few weeks, you will either receive a letter requesting more information or you will receive the dog's certification.

Missy is already certified as a therapy dog; however, occasional brush-up training can prevent mishaps.

11

What Problems Should You Foresee?

Problems?

In the eight years that I have been doing therapy dog work and in the six years that the Love on a Leash group has been working, there have been very few problems. Occasionally, there is a house-training accident. Once, a dog was overstressed and vomited. There was one scratch from a paw that wanted to be shaken, but no one has ever been bitten and no communicable diseases have ever been transmitted.

Many potential problems can be eliminated by taking care to train and socialize a therapy dog carefully. A thorough evaluation during therapy dog certification will point out any potential trouble spots, and continuing education for both the dog and his owner can help prevent trouble from surfacing later.

Prevention is ongoing. Be aware that problems can occur. It is your job to prevent them from happening.

Always Carry a Plastic Bag

When working with animals of any kind, the most commonly seen accident is related to house-training. Some dogs relieve themselves when they are stressed—no matter *where* they are. Clean up the mess as quickly as possible, then try to determine what prompted the behavior. Was the dog introduced to the facility and its residents too quickly? If you think this is a problem, visit fewer people at a time and shorten the length of the visits. As the dog gains more confidence, his stress (and problem behavior) should disappear.

Some experienced therapy dogs, knowing that a visit is pending, may not take the time to relieve themselves when given a chance. They'd rather visit as soon as possible! Train your dog so that he understands that he is not allowed to visit until he has at least tried to relieve himself.

Many times, a reluctant dog will relieve himself if taken to a spot where another dog has already been. Point to the spot and in an encouraging voice tell your dog, "Go

A potty break outside, before a visit, can help prevent "accidents."

Potty!" or whatever your command may be. When he goes, praise him.

Even if your dog has already relieved himself, *always* carry a plastic bag. The Love on a Leash group has a saying that is bounced around constantly: If you have a bag, you won't need it. If you forgot your bag, you will need one.

Use the plastic bag to pick up a stool. If the dog urinates, blot it up as best you can and notify the housekeeping staff immediately.

If you have a male dog that likes to lift his leg, *watch him* at all times. Correct him if he evens *looks* like he might lift his leg. Keep in mind that some elderly patients may have their own accidents and your dog may react to this. Pay attention.

Protect the People You Are Visiting

Every therapy dog must have self-control. Dogs are perfectly capable of restraining themselves when excited; it happens every day. However, this is a learned behavior. If your dog jumps on people, bounces around uncontrollably, or expresses too much excitement, he cannot visit until he learns control. You cannot risk injuring or frightening the people you are visiting.

One of the easiest ways to teach self-control to a dog is to teach him to sit. If your dog learns that he must sit for everything he wants, including food, treats, petting, the tennis ball, and greeting the neighbor, he will begin to sit automatically when he wants something. If he's sitting, he cannot be jumping.

Another way to teach your dog to concentrate on his behavior is to leave his leash on whenever you can supervise him. If he's in the house with you, let him drag his leash. If you are out in the backyard with him, let him drag his leash. Watch him, of course, because you don't want the leash to get tangled on something and choke him. Your

*Ursa is invited into the couch by Lenore, but she
must still mind her manners and be gentle.*

dog will look on the leash as a control tool. By putting it on
him, you are reminding him to control himself.

The leash also allows you to get hold of him quickly. If
he misbehaves and tries to keep out of your reach, don't try
to grab him. Simply step on the end of the leash. If he
dashes away, he corrects himself. When you have stopped
his forward movement, take hold of the leash and follow
through with your training.

Injuries

The skin of the elderly can be very fragile and dog claws
can tear it. It's your responsibility to make sure that your
dog doesn't hurt anyone. Always work to prevent injury.

Bites are another catastrophe. Any animal is capable of biting under the right circumstances. Your dog should be screened for proper temperament, and trained and socialized to prevent any biting behavior. Never, *ever* leave your dog unattended. If you must go to the restroom, take him with you. If you need to make a telephone call, ask a caretaker a question, whatever, *take your dog with you.* Watch him at all times.

A good way to prevent biting is to *know your dog.* Dogs usually bite when they feel fear. It is their reaction to protect themselves. Therefore, know the situations in which your dog might get nervous. Know how much handling he can take so you can give him a break before he gets stressed. Protect him if residents' hands get too rough or if someone is squeezing him too hard. If someone is too rough, step in politely and rescue your dog without hurting the resident's feelings, "Fido needs a short break. Let me have him and I'll send someone else in to visit with you, okay?"

If your dog scratches or bites a resident, don't try to hide it. The wound must be immediately washed and dressed, even if it looks minor. Notify a caregiver immediately and then notify the activities director. If the injury was a bite, management will want to reaffirm that your dog has had his rabies shot.

After the initial formalities are underway, evaluate your dog's behavior. Look for the triggering event so that you can avoid it (and prevent another biting incident).

Communicable Health Problems

Researchers have identified approximately seventy zoonotic diseases that can be transmitted from pets to humans. However, the incidences of anything actually being transmitted are very rare. Make every effort to ensure that your dog is healthy. People with compromised immune systems can be vulnerable to diseases, as can the very young or the elderly.

The New York State Veterinary Medical Association has recommended that AIDS patients have their pets screened for parasites and fungal or bacterial infections twice a year, as AIDS patients can be susceptible to health problems caused by these agents.

Establish a good working relationship with your veterinarian. Make sure he understands the type of people you visit. He may even wish to speak to the facility's physician. Follow the health-care and maintenance guidelines he establishes. If he feels that a quarterly fecal flotation is needed, do it. If he recommends a particular schedule of vaccinations, follow it. Make sure you understand what he is recommending and why.

Allergies

Allergies can be much more serious than a runny nose or a rash. Allergies can be life threatening. If someone says that he is allergic to animals, take his word for it and stay away from him.

The activities director should identify those people allergic to animal dander and make sure they are not involved in any group visits. You should also know who these people are (so that you can avoid them) and know which rooms to avoid when visiting from room to room.

Be Prepared—Anything Can Happen!

Preparation, care, and common sense can prevent most accidents. The hardest part is to not become complacent. If an accident has never happened, it's easy to think that it never will. *Always* watch your dog.

Appendix:
Is a Resident Therapy Dog Right
for Your Facility?

Love on a Leash was written for all potential owners of therapy dogs. This appendix, however, addresses a specific group of readers: facility directors who are contemplating whether or not to purchase a *resident* therapy dog.

The primary difference between visiting therapy dogs and resident dogs is the number of hours the dogs are available to the residents. Obviously, visiting dogs are available only during visits—usually two hours, two to three times a month. The resident dog, however, is at the facility twenty-four hours a day.

Adding a resident therapy dog to a facility is more than simply getting a dog somewhere and turning it loose in the facility. A therapy dog requires a major commitment of money, time, and effort on the part of the facility's management and the staff. Then, the dog must be carefully chosen, trained, introduced to the residents, and supervised.

Should Your Facility Have a Therapy Dog?

The decision to add a therapy dog to your staff must be considered carefully from every possible angle, because it is a commitment for the life of the dog. It would be cruel, both to the residents and the dog, to introduce a dog, train him, have him begin working at the facility, and then take him away.

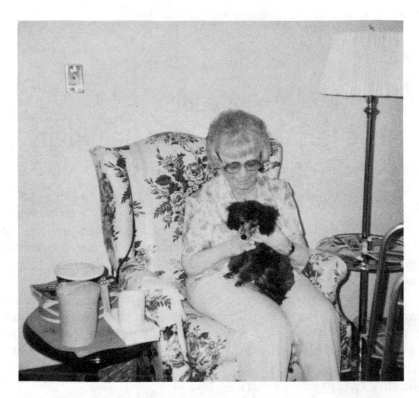

Only when the dog is totally trustworthy in regard to his behavior should he be allowed free run of the facility.

You need to consider the funding required to obtain and support a therapy dog: the cost of the dog, the dog's facilities, yearly vaccinations, initial spay or neuter, food, daily care, emergency veterinary costs, grooming, training, certification fees, and insurance.

You will need to assign a minimum of three staff members to care for the dog—a primary care person and two relief staff members for hours when the primary care person is off work or on vacation. All of these people must be familiar with dogs, dog care and training, and, most importantly, must be willing to do the job. Some facilities have added care of the dog to the job descriptions of the staff member/dog caretaker.

Is a Resident Therapy Dog Right for Your Facility? ——— 141

Sample Job Description
Caretaker of Resident Therapy Dog

Job Title   Caretaker for Residential Therapy Pet

Job Summary   Implement and coordinate care for residential pets to be used to develop social, recreational, and intellectual skills for the residents. Coordinate use of animals with other staff members as needed.

Special Requirements   Knowledge of care and needs of pets. Able to supervise and train such animals.

Job Duties

1. Screen and acquire suitable pets for the facility. Coordinate acquisitions with management.

2. Provide care for the pets to maintain good physical and mental health, which includes providing veterinary care, exercise/play, meals and treats, and grooming. Maintain all care records.

3. Provide or arrange for training for each animal as needed.

4. Introduce pets to the staff and supervise all visits.

5. Coordinate use of pets as therapy givers with staff. Coordinate events around daily residential activities. Ensure one-on-one contact with residents as needed.

6. Arrange for residents' families to meet each pet.

It is important that there is an enthusiastic consensus for adding a resident dog. If the staff is not enthusiastic, you should consider having visiting therapy dogs come in on a regular basis instead.

The residents must also want a dog. If there are a large number of people who are allergic to dogs, unresponsive, or critically ill, perhaps an aquarium or a few caged birds in the recreation room would be better than a dog. For the dog to do his work, people must want to interact with him.

If the residents want a dog, the staff agrees to work with and care for the dog, and management agrees to fund it, a resident therapy dog will work wonders.

Things to Consider Before Buying a Dog

It may seem like a formidable task to decide whether or not a resident therapy dog will work for your facility. Granted, it is not a decision to make lightly. However, the answers to the two questions presented in the following pages—Where will your dog live? and What does your dog need?—will give you a clear indication of the space, equipment, and other resources needed to provide a "happy home" for your resident dog.

Where Will Your Dog Live?

Your therapy dog will need a fenced-in run, preferably one that is accessed by a pet door so that he can come and go as he pleases. "Accidents" can be prevented this way. The run does not have to be big. In fact, six feet wide by twenty feet long is wonderful. The easiest surface to clean is concrete, although concrete can get hot in the summer. A grassy area will work as well, except that it will also have to be maintained. The best fencing is either solid wood or chain link, six feet high.

Your dog will also need a bed inside the facility, where he can get away from residents if he wishes, and a place where he will be fed. If the run is located off the activity director's office, your dog's bed and dishes could be placed in this office. This way, the activity director can supervise the dog, his care, and the cleaning of the run. The dog can be closed into the office, too, if necessary.

Daily exercise is a must for all dogs, but it's even more important for a working dog. Exercise uses up excess energy that might otherwise cause the dog to get into mischief and it also allows the dog to have fun, stretch his muscles, and relieve stress.

What Does Your Dog Need?

In addition to the run and his bed, your dog will need some other supplies, including food and water dishes, a brush and comb, a pooper scooper, and a trash can for dog feces disposal.

Dog food is also needed, of course. The type of food used will probably depend on what he was fed previously or what your veterinarian suggests. If you change his food abruptly, he will probably get an upset stomach, even diarrhea. This is an awful way for him to be introduced to the facility. Keep him on the same food for a while and then, if you wish to change it, do so gradually, over a period of several weeks.

Place a pet care chart in a specific location, perhaps in the activity director's office, to document the dog's daily care. Has he been brushed, walked, trained, fed, and watered? Has his run been cleaned? Has someone played with him? Have the responsible staff members sign the chart as each activity is completed. This ensures that your dog is properly cared for, yet chores are not needlessly duplicated.

You can also post your dog's schedule next to the care chart. Dogs are creatures of habit and your dog will be much happier when he eats, plays, walks, visits, and goes outside on a regular schedule. However, your dog's daily routine and the facility's can be coordinated. When does the primary-care staff member start work? The dog can be fed after she checks in. The dog can be taken out for a walk or playtime during a slow time in the afternoon when many residents are napping.

Choosing the Right Dog

The activities director and/or the person responsible for the dog should be involved in choosing your therapy dog. Don't hesitate to contact a local dog trainer for advice on selecting a dog. Explain what you are doing and the kind of dog you need. Indicate the type of training and certification your dog requires.

Don't be in a hurry to get just any dog. Choose the dog carefully. The guidelines in Chapter 4 apply to resident therapy dogs as well as visiting therapy dogs, except that a resident therapy dog should be between one and two years of age. If he is younger, he will require considerable supervision as he outgrows his puppy ways. If he's too much older, he will have a shorter working life.

RESIDENT THERAPY PET
CARE SHEET

Date_____

Pet's Name_____ Breed/Species_____

Primary Caretaker_____

Shift (Circle one)

8 A.M.- Noon   Noon - 4 P.M.   4 P.M.- 8 P.M.   8 P.M.- 8 A.M.

FED / WATERED

TIME	INITIALS

GROOMED

TIME	INITIALS

RELIEVED

TIME	INITIALS

PLAY / EXERCISE

TIME	INITIALS

RUN CLEANED

TIME	INITIALS

FOOD / SUPPLIES CHECKED

TIME	INITIALS

Search for the right dog at humane societies or shelters, from breeders, groomers, trainers, or even classified ads in the local newspaper. Many excellent resident therapy dogs have been dogs that failed guide dog or service dog school. The dog may not have been quite up to par, for whatever reason, to work as a guide dog or service dog, but yet is still a well-trained, well-socialized dog that would make a great resident therapy dog.

When you have located a potential therapy dog, arrange to meet him in a place that he does not consider his territory. Take someone with you to see him, preferably someone with experience with dogs. Conduct the following tests and have the other person observe and take notes. Make sure you record everything, because if you look at several dogs, you may confuse their reactions.

Walk up to the dog and extend your hand for the dog to sniff. What is his reaction? If he approaches you and sniffs, good. If he holds his ground while you approach, good. If he growls, bares teeth, lifts his lips, raises his hackles, or backs away from you, cross him off your list. He's not qualified to be a therapy dog.

If the dog has allowed you to approach him, attempt to pet him. Place your hand on his head and run your hand over his head, around his ears, and down his neck. Run both of your hands over his body, and down his legs and tail. Does he seem to enjoy it? Is he rolling over for you to rub his tummy? Is he trying to get you to play? Is he trying to climb into your lap? If so, good. If he growls at any time, bares his teeth, raises his hackles, pulls away or tries to walk away, cowers, or urinates, disqualify him.

If the dog is still in the running, pet him some more but handle him a bit roughly. (If he is going to be exposed to kids, what will he do if a child climbs on top of him? If elderly people will be petting him, what will he do if crippled hands hug him tightly?) Again, eliminate him from consideration if he growls, bares his teeth, or tries to pull away.

If the dog is still in consideration, have your associate drop a clipboard to the floor to test the dog's sound sensitivity and reaction to unexpected noises. Drop a walker or wheelchair over on its side. How did the dog react? If he notices or goes to investigate, that's good. If he is startled but then turns to look, that's okay. However, if he tries to run away, urinates, freezes, or cowers, eliminate him from consideration.

Assess the dog's manners. Is he rowdy? Does he jump on people? Does he bounce on the furniture? Does he pull on the leash? Training can solve undesirable behavior, but if the dog already knows basic manners and obedience commands, it will be much easier to incorporate him into the facility.

If this dog is still a viable option after you have performed these tests, take him to a veterinarian for a complete physical. Tell the vet the type of dog for which you are looking and the training he must complete. Ask for his professional opinion. First, is the dog healthy? Second, can he physically do the job?

When the dog gets the okay from the veterinarian, take the dog to the facility for a test visit. How does he react to the residents? Is he put off by grabbing hands? How does he walk on the slippery floor? Do wheelchairs spook him? How do the staff members react to him?

When the dog meets all of your criteria, as well as the guidelines in Chapter 4, meet with facility management and anyone else having to work with the dog and make a joint decision about acquiring the dog. Review all of your data. Make a responsible decision based on which dog responded best to the tests.

Bringing the Dog "Home"

Once you have selected the dog that is right for your facility, there are a couple different ways you can handle his initial training. Some facilities put the dog in a foster home while he is trained. If the dog has already had some training and is basically well mannered, bring him "home" and conduct his training at your facility. What you do depends on the training skills of the staff members involved and the trainer that you have hired to assist you (if necessary).

*Much of the training for the residential dog and the visiting dog
is the same. Ursa is trained to sit next to the wheelchair
to be readily accessible for petting.*

Help your dog get to know the layout of the facility.
Show him his run and pet door. Let him see where he will
eat and sleep. Let the trainer know if there are any
restricted areas in which the dog is not allowed.

Introducing Your Dog to the Residents

The residents should be told that you are looking for a
therapy dog so that when you get one they are not surprised

by him. Change is difficult for many people and advance notice helps alleviate some of the shock, especially for residents who might be leery of the idea or afraid of dogs.

Your resident therapy dog should be on leash the first few weeks after he joins the facility. On leash, he can be restrained if he gets overly excited and he can be led from resident to resident. In the beginning, keep his visits through the facility short—maybe a half hour. Then, take him back to his sleeping area and have him lay down or let him go outside to relieve himself. An hour or so later, take him visiting again for another half an hour. By keeping his forays short, you will keep him from getting overwhelmed, frightened, or too excited. Very gradually, over several weeks, lengthen his visits.

By taking him back to his bed, you are teaching him that this is the place where he can get away from things, away from the residents and the noises of the facility. Residents and other staff members should not disturb him when he is in his bed. Being with a lot of people twenty-four hours a day, every day, can become very stressful. The area in which his bed is located should be off limits so that he can have time alone.

Introduce your dog to the residents one by one: "Margaret, this is Jake. Jake, this is Margaret." This introduction shows respect for your residents, tells them the dog's name in a manner they understand, and, believe it or not, many dogs are very capable of learning to recognize people's names. If the names are repeated each time the dog sees the person, he will begin to associate that name with that particular person.

When introducing your resident therapy dog, always ask the residents if they want to pet him. Some people get pleasure out of simply watching the dog. Others want to pet and hug him. Let the residents set the pace of the visit. However, be prepared to intervene if a resident gets too rough.

Don't take the dog off leash during his visits or allow him free run of the facility until he is under verbal control and is thoroughly trained so that he won't jump on people, paw, or scratch. Many dogs take a month or more to integrate into a facility, so don't be discouraged if his progress seems to be slow in certain areas. If he is having difficulty learning certain commands (such as not climbing into residents' laps) or following guidelines (such as not raiding trash cans) talk to a trainer and ask for help in correcting these problems.

Using Your Resident Therapy Dog

Your dog can offer his services in a variety of ways. When under control and well mannered, he can be allowed free run of the facility to visit people as he pleases, giving them comfort, attention, and love. He may nap in the recreation room, giving comfort by simply being there. Or he may wander the halls with a tennis ball, looking for someone to throw it for him.

The activities director can use him by scheduling dog shows that allow the residents to watch his training sessions or show off new skills or tricks. The activities director can also make sure that he is visiting the people that request to see him and he is seeing the people that seem to need him the most.

Physical therapists can use him to motivate their patients. Throwing the tennis ball for him uses muscles, as does brushing him. If your dog walks nicely on the leash without pulling, more agile residents can walk him up and down the hall or even around the block, which is therapeutic, good exercise, and enjoyable. Therapists can even use the dog to demonstrate the exercise they want a resident to learn. For example, they might ask your dog to lay down and then manipulate one of his legs, so that the patient laughs and cooperates more willingly with her own exercises.

Psychologists and counselors can use your dog as an aid to get over an emotional rough spot. Grief counselors can use him to offer comfort and love.

Encourage staff members to try things with the dog. If an idea works, wonderful! Use it again. If it doesn't, try something else. Each dog and each facility must find out what works for them.

Liz Palika and Ursa, her Australian Shepherd.

About the Author

Liz Palika has been involved in therapy dog work since the mid-1980s and is the founder of the Foundation for Pet Provided Therapy of which Love on a Leash is a part. Liz and her three Australian Shepherds—Care Bear, Ursa, and Dax—have accumulated thousands of hours in nursing homes, retirement homes, day-care centers, and special education classrooms.

Liz has been teaching dog obedience classes since the mid-1970s and is a member of the National Association of Dog Obedience Instructors, endorsed for all levels of obedience training. She is also a professional member of the Association of Pet Dog Trainers.

Liz is also a member of Dog Writers Association of America and has written several books about dogs, dog training, and other pets. Her book *Fido, Come! Training Your Dog with Love and Understanding* was nominated by Dog Writers as Best Training Book of 1994. Her book *Australian Shepherd: Champion of Versatility* won the coveted Maxwell Award from Dog Writers as Best Breed Book of 1995. Liz has also been writing for *Dog Fancy* magazine since 1985. She has also had articles published in *Newsweek, Dog World, Cat Fancy,* and other publications.

Liz currently lives in California with her three dogs and is working on her twelfth book.

Bibliography

Arkow, Phil. *Pet Therapy: A Study of the Use of Companion Animals in Selected Therapies.* Colorado Springs, CO: The Humane Society of the Pikes Peak Region, 1982.

Arkow, Phil. *How to Start a Pet Therapy Program.* Colorado Springs, CO: The Humane Society of the Pikes Peak Region, (no date).

Barnett, Joan, and Joseph Quigley. "Animals in Long Term Care Facilities: A Framework for Program Planning." *Journal of Long Term Care Administration* vol. 12, no. 4 (Winter 1984): 1–8.

Beck, Alan, and Aaron Katcher. *Between Pets and People.* New York: Putnam Publishing, 1983.

Bernard, Shari, and Cristyl Chance. "The Utilization of Animals as a Therapeutic Modality." *Occupational Therapy Forum* vol. III, no. 29 (July 1988): 1–3.

Burch, Mary R. *Volunteering With Your Pet.* New York: Howell Book House, 1996.

Carmack, Betty J. "The Role of Companion Animals for Persons With AIDS/HIV." *Holistic Nursing Practice* vol. 5, no. 2 (January 1991): 24–31.

Carmack, Betty J. "Pet Loss and the Elderly." *Holistic Nursing Practice* vol. 5, no. 2 (January 1991): 80–87.

Carmack, Betty J., and Debra Fila. "Animal-Assisted Therapy: A Nursing Intervention." *Nursing Management* vol. 20, no. 5 (May 1989): 96–101.

Cousins, Norman. *Anatomy of An Illness*. New York: W. W. Norton, 1979.

Cousins, Norman. *The Healing Heart*. New York: Avon Books, 1984.

Davis, Kathy Diamond. "What Rules Do We Really Need for Therapy Dogs?" *Alpha Bits* vol. 7, no. 1 (March 1996): 3.

Davis, Kathy Diamond. *Therapy Dogs*. New York: Howell Book House, 1992.

Delta Society. The *Handbook for Animal-Assisted Activities and Animal-Assisted Therapy*. Renton, WA: The Delta Society, 1991.

Fogle, Bruce. *Pets and People*. New York: Viking Press, 1984.

Francis, Gloria M. "Here Come the Puppies: The Power of the Human-Animal Bond." *Holistic Nursing Practice* vol. 5, no. 2 (January 1991): 38–41.

Friedmann, E., et al. "Animal Companions and One-Year Survival of Patients After Discharge From a Coronary Care Unit." *Public Health Reports* vol. 95, no. 4 (1995): 305–312.

Hart, Lynette A. "Pets and Your Health" in *The World Book of Health & Medical Annual*. Chicago: World Book, 1995.

Hart, Lynette A. "Dogs as Human Companions: A Review of the Relationship." In *The Domestic Dog*. Cambridge: Cambridge University Press, 1995.

Lee, Ronnal L., et al. *Guidelines: Animals in Nursing Homes*. Renton, WA: The Delta Society, 1991.

Levinson, Boris M. *Pets and Human Development*. Springfield, MO: Charles C. Thomas, 1972.

Levinson, Boris M. "Pets and Personality." *Psychological Reports* no. 42 (1978): 1031–1038.

Loney, Jan. "The Canine Therapist in a Residential Children's Setting: Qualifications, Recruitment, Training and Related Matters." *Journal of the American Academy of Child Psychiatry* vol. 10, no. 3 (1971): 518–523.

Lorenz, Konrad. *Man Meets Dog*. Middlesex, England: Penguin Books, 1953.

McCulloch, Michael J. "Companion Animals, Human Health, and the Veterinarian." In *Textbook of Veterinary Internal Medicine.* Stephen J. Ettinger, ed. Philadelphia: W. B. Saunders, 1983: 228–235.

Palika, Liz. *Fido, Come! Training Your Dog with Love and Understanding.* Wilsonville, OR: Doral Publishing, 1993.

Pryor, Karen. *Don't Shoot the Dog!* New York: Bantam Books, 1985.

Root, Jacqueline P. *K-9 Therapy Group.* Fairfax, VA: Denlinger Publishers, 1990.

Ruckert, Janet. *The Four-Footed Therapist.* Berkeley: Ten Speed Press, 1987.

Schantz, Peter M. "Preventing Potential Health Hazards Incidental to the Use of Pets in Therapy." *Anthrozoos* vol. IV, no. 1: 14–23.

Selye, Hans. *The Stress of Life.* New York: McGraw-Hill, 1976.

Shaffer, Martin. *Life After Stress.* Chicago: Contemporary Books, 1983.

Stiverson, Carla, and Gary Dodson. *Assistance Dog Providers in the United States.* Muncie, IN: Ball State University, 1995.

Van Remoorlene, Lihane. "Therapeutic Effects of Animals for Children With Special Needs." *People-Animals-Environment* (Spring 1988): 23–28.

Other Sources of Information

It is important to have your dog certified by one of the nationally (or internationally) recognized therapy dog certification organizations. Not only will this offer you and your dog public recognition, but it also shows that your dog has been trained, evaluated, and certified as a therapy dog. These organizations also offer liability insurance for you and your dog during your visits. These groups have newsletters that promote communication between therapy dog handlers and regularly publish educational articles for your continuing education.

All of the organizations listed here have members all over the country, and most have organized chapters or groups. When you write for information about certifying your dog, ask if there is a therapy dog group in your area. If there isn't, think about starting your own. Activities are always more fun when you share them with other people.

There are also many small therapy dog groups formed by dog trainers, dog-training clubs, kennel clubs, and Humane Society volunteers. To find a group, call the pet professionals in your area. Most of these groups require that their members certify their dogs through one of the national organizations.

The Delta Society
321 Burnett Avenue South
Renton, WA 98055
1-800-869-6898 (V/TDD)

Love on a Leash,
A Division of the Foundation for Pet Provided Therapy
3809 Plaza Drive, No. 107–309
Oceanside, CA 92056
619-630-4824

St. Johns Ambulance Therapy Dogs
1199 Deyell 3rd Line
Millbrook, Ontario
Canada L0A 1G0
705-932-3626

Therapy Dog International, Inc.
6 Hilltop Road
Mendham, NJ 07945
201-543-0888

Therapy Dogs, Inc.
2416 East Fox Farm Road
Cheyenne, WY 82007
307-638-3223

Your Comments are Invited

If you enjoyed *Love on a Leash*, we would like to hear from you. If you want to comment on any aspect of the book, feel free to do so. Just write:

> Editorial Office
> Alpine Publications
> 225 S. Madison Ave.
> Loveland, CO 80537

For a Free Catalog of Alpine Books

or for information on other Alpine Blue Ribbon titles, please write to our Customer Service Department, P. O. Box 7027, Loveland, Colorado 80537, or call toll free 1-800-777-7257.

Additional ALPINE Titles of Interest:

K - 9 Therapy Groups: Organization and Management
J. Root
How to organize your own group, recruit, train, schedule, and more.

Living With Small and Toy Dogs
T. Jester
Toy dogs *are* different. Learn how to understand, discipline, and train them.

Owner's Guide to Better Behavior in Dogs
W. Campbell
An excellent book on dog behavior, correcting or preventing problem behavior, communicating with your dog, and more.

The Mentally Sound Dog
G. Clark and W. Boyer
Another approach to dog behavior and developing a sound personality, dealing with problem behavior, and more.